Waiting for the Goats

Life and Death in a Bulgarian Village

Christopher Fenton

Fimber Press

First published by Fimber Press in 2025

English translation of Geo Milev 'September' reproduced with
kind permission from Tom Phillips and Worple Press

ISBN No. 978-1-0683743-0-2

These stories are based on real events.
The names have been changed.

Cover design by geneva_art
Fimber Press logo design by Pinar Yildiz

www.christopherfentonwritings.com
instagram: christopherfentonwritings

www.Fimberpress.co.uk

To Claire,

my sweet pea and partner in adventure

Contents

"I do not know certainty. At best I deal in possibilities."

Renato Cacciopoli
(Mathematician)

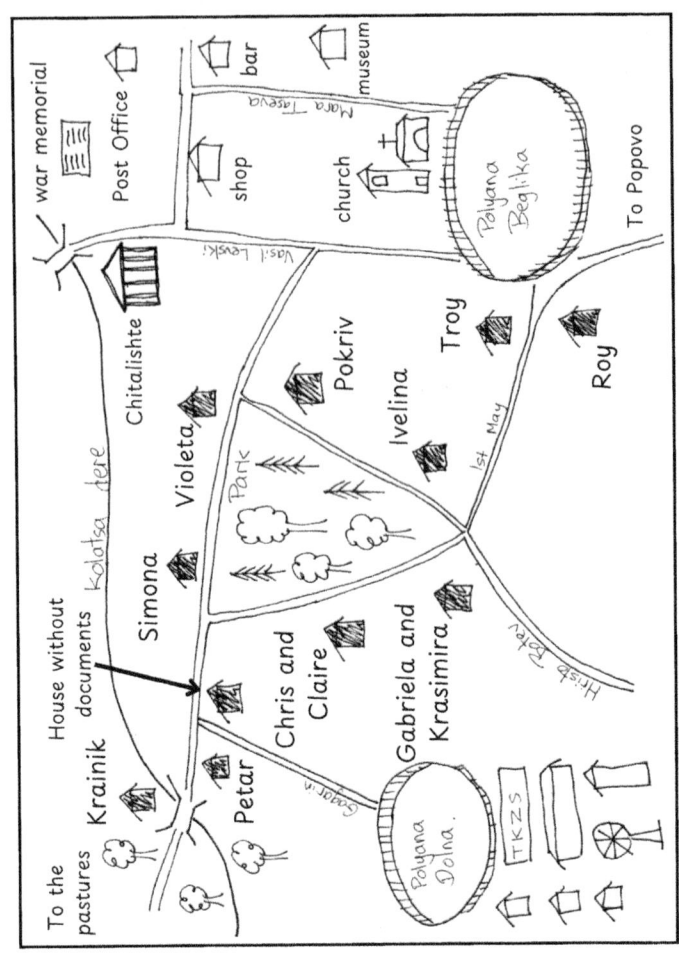

Podgoritsa village showing the neighbourhood around the park. The house without documents is where we waited for the goats.

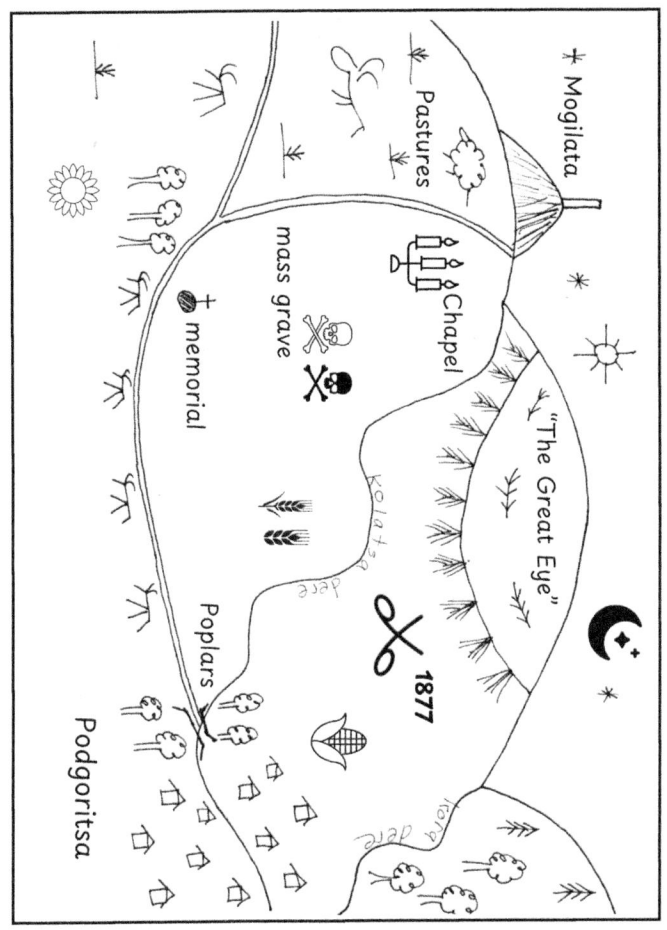

Landscape to the west of the village of Podgoritsa showing the pastures where the goats walked every day and the *mogila* that featured in so many of the tales. The Great Eye very rarely opened.

Prelude
Podgoritsa, Bulgaria 2011

Violeta was sitting in her usual place on the window ledge. On cold days like this, she carried an old sack and laid it on the stone as she talked to her friend Simona who was crouched as usual under the mulberry tree. After six months in the village, we already had two goats and every morning I waited with Violeta and Simona for the shepherd to come. These two women became our closest friends and as we waited, they told stories about the village that stood here before the ruins.

The empty brick house had gaping windows and the metal door of the fusebox creaked open like a ghost. In the distance, we could see the hills above the Cherni Lom, the river that flowed from Popovo to Gagovo, then on to the Lom and the great Danube itself. When they heard Radiana's cows on the other side of the stream, Simona and

Violeta stopped talking for a minute. I looked over to the ploughed field to see the sheep and goats heading down the track where the battle had been. By now, the sun had disappeared behind the ridge and the great mound, *mogilata*, was etched in light. In 1877, during the Russian-Turkish war, the Cossacks were entrenched up there for four days before retreating to Byala when the Turkish cavalry overwhelmed them on the field.

If neglected, it was their neat little roofs that went first but some of the mud brick walls around the gardens were still in good order. On Spring days, Baba Gabriela used to come out with a bucket of clay paint to refresh her sections. Once the tiles slipped, the rain got in, washing away paint and plaster and eroding the silt at the heart of each handmade brick. The house on the corner had been empty for years and the neglected garden walls were nothing but tall pillars of mud. The roof beams tilted down inside the carcass of the building like the bones of a dead beast.

Time had stopped dead because none of us knew when the goats would come back. Sometimes we waited for an hour or more. As they talked, I tried to catch every word but could never find them in the language books. The two women used a Bulgarian dialect only heard in this village and many of the terms and phrases went back to Ottoman times. They explained each story with a hand gesture, pointing directly across the lane or vaguely far away to the other side of the hill. The words were at one with the place and had no meaning without the geography that contained them. They seemed to bubble up out of the ground like water from a spring.

'Do you know the story of Antola?' Simona said. 'When the men were building our house, they took me up onto the scaffold and I showed them the view towards *mogilata*, the mound. After that they used to sit up there by themselves and think about the young girl tied to the stake in her wedding dress.'

Wherever I went, I could see the earthen barrow that Simona loved to talk about. From far away, it was a tiny lump on the long horizon, a beacon that drew me back to the village. The great mound had history. In 1937 the Bulgarian army had used it as a signal point when King Boris himself inspected the troops stationed up there. But Simona did not talk about that. What she remembered was the legend of the Princess. She told the story with pride, describing how Antola went behind her father's back to be with the boy she loved. Then her face became serious as she sat there on the bench, feeling for ticks around the furry neck of one of her cats. They never stayed still for long and when the cat jumped out of her grasp, she wiped her hands together and told me the final piece of the tale.

'When he discovered the truth, the King staged a mock wedding up there with a white dress and white horses and tied her to a pole and all of the soldiers mounded up the soil around the King's daughter and slowly buried her alive.'

Then she added some words of her own, 'The poor lamb.'

1

Winter is Coming

On the long journey east, back in 2010, Wally the dog slept on his bed in the back of the truck as we trundled through the *Schengen* countries. All the way from Rotterdam to Vienna there were no checkpoints, but once we left Austria, the frontiers came back. First Hungary, then Romania and finally Bulgaria, which on this orientation was the last country in Europe.

Wally never saw Barnsley again because, five years after we arrived in the village, he wandered off into the forest and did not come back. We assumed that he died out there in some favoured spot, choosing his own resting place without a grave or marker. We never found him and sometimes I think that I might want to do the same one day, just walk away, lie myself down in the dry oak leaves and melt slowly into the Balkan soil.

At Fratesti, the Romanian police flagged us down for speeding and that was quite an achievement in a vehicle with a top speed of 70 kmh. It took our minds off the approaching Bulgarian border, so when Claire and I finally arrived at the Danube Bridge, we were not prepared. We hardly noticed the abandoned forecourts or the dogs that roamed around for scraps of bread and meatballs. The kind of unkempt Balkan disorder that we have grown used to, was something new at that stage, but we were too busy watching the uniformed men to notice it. On the tarmac, four Bulgarian customs guards were staring and pointing at the truck.

The Danube is the greatest river in Europe and flows through some of the world's most beautiful cities. Once its waters have passed Hungary and Serbia, the growing river flows for 370 km as the border between Romania and Bulgaria. In 2010, when Claire, Wally and myself journeyed east, there was only one place you could cross, making the checkpoint at Giurgiu a bottleneck for trucks heading for Turkey and Asia. The border is more than just a physical barrier because it marks the divide between two languages. Romanian is close to Italian whereas Bulgarian is Slavic, similar to Russian and uses the Cyrillic alphabet. In Romanian you count from one to five like this, *unu, doi, trei, patru, cinci,* but on the other side in Bulgaria it is like this, *edno, dve, tri, cheteri, pet.* As we drove across the bridge, Wally sat on the bed looking out of the window at the wild border dogs, whilst Claire and I stared down through the girders of the bridge at the mixing waters. At that stage we did not know how long we would be staying. A large sign above the road read българия. There were no cute slogans, not even a word of welcome. As soon as we saw the indecipherable Cyrillic letters, we knew we had some studying to do.

It was the end of a hot summer. On the Bulgarian side of the bridge we waited, unsure whether to join the line of lorries or stay with the shiny black saloon cars. The vehicle which had served its time as a library bus and trundled around the pit villages of South Yorkshire had been our home for six months. When two of the border guards finally made a move and climbed in, they stepped back in shock. Wally was looking at them from the bed but it was not the dog they had come to inspect. They studied our pot belly stove for some time, then went outside and smoked a couple of cigarettes on the hot tarmac, pointing up at the battered metal flue, the chimney that stuck out of the roof. One of them took off his cap, crusted with gold braid and badges and wiped the sweat from his forehead. He got on the phone and summoned two more officers with slightly different uniforms. We had been waiting in the heat for an hour, but nobody had yet given us permission to enter the country.

'Maybe it's a health and safety thing?' I whispered from behind the curtain, but before Claire had time to answer, the four men climbed back on board. In thick leather belts with pistols on the hip, they filled the small space between stove, kitchen and bed. After more discussion, they edged back out down the steps, saying nothing. Finally, the last one of the men to leave noticed our worried faces and smiled, speaking politely in perfect English,

'Don't be concerned,' he said, 'I think my colleague should get a stove like that for his fishing caravan. He wants to know how it should be insulated. If you are planning to live in this bus, you will definitely be needing that *petchka* when the snow comes. It's going to be a cold winter.'

'Snow? But it's August,' I said.

'Yes of course it is but winter is coming. Winter is always coming,' and he handed back our passports and waved us through.

Petchka - wood stove. I made a mental note of my first Bulgarian word.

The GPS display showed only the main roads with empty green spaces between the towns so we unfolded the map, bought from a petrol station on the edge of Ruse. Then we took the long route, driving slowly down the pot-holed back lanes. The village signs had Slavic names in Cyrillic that were almost impossible to decipher; горско абланово Gorsko Ablanovo .... Крепча Krepcha ..... кацелово Katselovo.... When we asked for the town of Popovo, the people in the streets made a hand signal pointing the way ahead. Then they got back to work. It was the same in every village. Plastic sheets were spread out on the hot tarmac. Men and women hitting bean pods with wooden hay forks. Some had already gathered together piles of clean white beans. In one place we stopped to take photos and a grand-daughter explained to us in English that they were harvesting the *bob*, which she pronounced as *bop*, like a dance.

'When will you eat them?' I shouted from the cab over the diesel grumble of the van, feeling dizzy from the adventure of it all.

'In winter,' she replied, 'They all have to be ready,' and she pointed to her older relatives. 'But not me. I live in Berlin,' she shouted after us and grinned. 'No need for winter in Berlin, just good vibes and techno,' and then she pulled a funny face and pumped her fist in the hot dry air.

I was still thinking like a nomad. A traveller. A tourist. It did not occur to me that a year later when our first Bulgarian anniversary came around, we might also be threshing bean pods on the tarmac. Just like farmers do.

The guidebook explained on its opening page that Bulgaria was a rural country at heart with an agrarian spirit. *The Lonely Planet* insisted that if you go back two or three generations most people were peasant farmers. Winter was often long and harsh so getting in the produce to feed the family until the Spring had always been deeply ingrained in the national psyche.

As we crossed the Danube bridge, I knew so little of the place. I had heard the choral folk music on the 1986 album, *Le Mystère des Voix Bulgares* but I could not begin to imagine that I would soon be performing some of those songs myself, on the violin in theatres across the country. I had heard of the capital, Sofia through the football team CSKA and had even passed through the railway station, inter-railing to Greece when I was 17 but I was yet to learn that the city does not declare itself to visitors. Guidebooks for Sofia are not that useful because the best bars are hidden away in basements and do not appear in the listings. In summer, many of them close down because so many young Sofia residents go off to spend August by the Black Sea on the wild beaches. These are places where you string up a hammock in the shoreline forests or pitch a tent directly on the sand. The freedom is tenacious and even though it is constantly under threat from developers and politicians, thousands will camp for free, sleeping in hammocks by the shore every summer.

Beyond Sofia, the guidebook showed pictures of the old town of Veliko Tarnovo and the outdoor cafes of Plovdiv, with gorgeous photos of *shopska salata* and glasses of apricot *rakia*, but there is a lot more hidden from view if you care to look. It does not take long to notice the abandoned factories and the crumbling concrete all around. The greatest challenge for western visitors is to become accustomed to the general air of neglect, the aesthetics of abandonment. Many villages are half-ruined and this has a profound effect on visitors and residents alike. It gives the recent dead a real prominence because, on the door facing the street, most empty houses still carry the fading black ribbon pinned up for the last inhabitant who died. The one whose bed was never slept in again.

It was not always like this. The land has been at the crossroads between Europe and Asia for centuries and was part of the Roman, Byzantine, Bulgarian and Ottoman Empires. The country is crossed by migration routes between east and west and the towns and villages have always welcomed international travellers. In the last two thousand years, Jews, Armenians, Turks, Circassians, Tartars, Greeks, Arabs, Albanians, Romanians, and before them Goths, Huns, Celts, Thracians and Romans had all passed through or made this place their home. The recent influx of British visitors is just another wave in the long history of immigration.

A month after crossing the border, we parked the van at the edge of the village pastures and watched the sun set over the village of Podgoritsa. Dark green trees shrouded the settlement, concealing hundreds of houses with their straw-coloured rooves. The next day we were going to buy one. If all went well, this was to be our last night in the van and we sat on the step drawing out every second in the soft fading light as if we did not want it to happen too fast. It had been a long slow journey but now everything was about to move in super speed. It felt like we should take a breath before the new adventure began so we watched the tiny flies dancing in the haze and the perfect clarity etched around its orange glare as the sun dipped out of sight.

Buying a house with a bundle of cash is terrifying when it's all the money you have but there was only one thought in my head as I drank my coffee that morning; the next day I would be waking up in a house, in a proper bed. There would be no more climbing up into the box we had built from salvaged palettes. I wondered how much I was going to miss our vehicle home. Just pushing open the folding door and smelling the stale diesel of the cab was enough. Enough to take me back to the day we drove up the steep hill to Fox Hagg Farm, near Sheffield. This was the caravan site where we lived on the edge of the Peak District, where Claire and I spent weeks stripping out the seats and then building the frame for the bed and the stove and the divan with storage underneath behind the driver's cab. We called upon some of the old industrial skills of Sheffield, enlisting help from backyard engineers and scrap dealers. Every part of the vehicle had its own story. The wood burner itself, we bought from a reclamation yard in Attercliffe and the silicon collar I found in a pipe depot near the Stocksbridge steelworks. It was a piece of magic that separated the hot metal chimney flue from the combustible material that housed the insulation in the ceiling of the truck.

For the solar panel, we went to a commune of eco-activists, in the moors above Huddersfield. They installed an inverter and battery inside which hooked up to the PV panel on the roof. We put so much effort into transforming the truck into a home that we forgot about the actual motor and for weeks ignored the fact that it needed an MOT inspection certificate. When we finally received this document, we treated it like a sacred text. The mechanic handed it over with some ceremony in front of all his colleagues at the entrance to the garage under the massive structure of the Wicker Arches. He said that he genuinely wished us well but did not expect to see this vehicle back for its renewal. A year later we sent him a postcard from the south of France. The van was still going strong and continued to do so throughout the epic trek that lay ahead of us.

As we left his yard a few days before we set off for London, he advised us, over the spluttering engine that, 'taking it steady', was the best chance we had. He was an optimist at heart and a bit of a philosopher. These were his final words,

'So, when it stops and gives up the dance, like we all must one day, just stay right there wherever you are, do not scrap this beast but use it as your home.'

At that point we had no way of knowing that his prophecy would come to pass in a remote corner of Bulgaria.

A year later, the van was still working. On the morning we were due to buy the house, we rattled along the broken road and stopped in the centre of Podgoritsa just to make sure we were doing the right thing. Claire was carrying a backpack full of money, leva notes withdrawn from the bank the day before. They would have to be counted out in front of the Notary before we could take possession of the keys. By signing the contract and legalizing the *Notarialen*

Akt we were saying, 'Yes!' to a new life. But was it too soon for us to let the old one go? It seemed important to remember every detail. Three men sat in a semi circle on old chairs, talking in the language we had spent the previous month trying to understand. A horse waited on the roadside, bothered by late summer flies, shaking its head and flapping the bright red tassle that hung between its eyes. Next to it, was a motorbike with a home-made side car that looked more like a coffin. We had parked up in so many beautiful corners of Europe and yet here we were, sitting on the steps of a battered war memorial. As I opened the beer bottle my eyes kept going back to the shattered concrete and the broken panes of glass. I knew Claire was asking herself the same thing,

'Was this really what we wanted? We had to stop somewhere eventually, we both knew that, but was this really the place?'

If we were being honest with ourselves, we had already made the decision to stay. During the previous month as we fed pigs, milked goats and tried to communicate with the shawled women on the back lanes, we both knew that this was it. It may not have been picturesque or cute, but it was everything we were looking for.

If ever there was a place where settled life would continue to be an adventure it was here. We could work according to our own rules, planting and digging and milking, and yet it was going to become much more than somewhere cheap to have a smallholding. Signing that contract would open the door to a whole new world.

That was our first day as residents of the village. Driving out of the square, Wally looked back from the window at the posters for the dead pasted up on the wall outside the mayor's office. I would see them for myself before long and very soon after that, the dead themselves.

2

A New Road

It suited us both, the nomadic way of life and I believe we could have stayed in the van forever, stepping lightly over the world. Volunteering on organic farms, we had been content to stay in one place for a few weeks but the day would always come when we woke up, ready to pack and move on. That was how things were but then our thinking began to change.

That winter on the road, as we travelled around France between the smallholdings, we watched our hosts carefully to see how they did it. Rolling new phrases like warm plum stones in our mouths, we sometimes spoke them out loud,

'Sour dough….. Compost…... Pickling jars…..'

As we rehearsed the tasks and activities, a plan was taking shape.

Up in the French Pyrenees we worked on a remote hill farm, *Le Mas de la Griffe*, which was about as far as you could go before hitting Spain. In the shadow of *Le Roc de France,* we slept in a shared yurt and worked long hours on the mountainside. After two weeks of carrying hay along rocky tracks, I stared down to the distant valley town of Amelie-les-Bains and began to dream of an imagined home. There was a cozy seat in the corner of the living room, cupboards in dark polished wood, a fire in the hearth, books on shelves and a winter woodstack. By the end of the six weeks on that farm, Claire and I were daring to talk about a place of our own where we could watch the seasons pass without working to anyone else's routine.

During the last week at *La Griffe*, we met Yavor. It was our first encounter with Bulgaria. Yavor Gabrovski had been a lumberjack in Sweden and a bodyguard in Munich but he held us captive with stories from the eastern bloc. He talked about the delicious food and the glorious mountains and the freedom of the sea coast.

'The Bulgarian Nature,' he would say and look around the faces in the firelight, drawing out the vowels of place-names as if they were something divine. He told us about the boredom of the 1980s and then the hope and chaos after the end of Communism and the beginning of something else. But every night we waited for the tales of the village, the place he remembered as a child, where they killed pigs at Christmas and made *rakia* from plums in backyard stills. He showed me on the map, tracing his finger from the source of the Danube in Germany all the way through Austria and Hungary, past the cities of Budapest and Bratislava deep into the land, which was still in my imagination a mysterious blank space beyond the iron curtain. Yavor explained,

'You must go from here, then all the way to here and then here.'

His finger flew over space and time from Serbia to Romania before it crossed the Danube to Bulgaria.

'Greece? No! Turkey? Forget it!' He declared.

Yavor told me that I knew nothing. In my head, Eastern Europe was one place. To cold war kids like me, for the Balkan states of the eastern bloc, there were no details or distinctions, just the fallout from Communism and whatever that was supposed to look like I had absolutely no idea.

The first thing we did, once we had taken possession of the keys was to bring inside Wally's bed and take down my violin from its hanging net. We had no clue where to put them so for days they sat together in the middle of the floor. After months living in a space the size of a small bedroom, the novelty of settees and beds, tables and chairs, solid walls and doors, turned the whole thing into another adventure. We had a sitting room the size of a tennis court, a kitchen with wood-fired *petchka*, huge oak beams that ran the length of the house and an outside staircase with worn wooden steps made from knotty planks. It was September so the garden was already filled with tomatoes, grapes, peaches and potatoes. Every time we opened a door, we found perfect pens for chickens and goats with water troughs carved from single blocks of stone. There was none of the brutalist concrete I had expected, for the architecture of the farm pre-dated the socialist years. The villages were far away from the factories and power stations. In houses like ours, they had been practising self-sufficiency for centuries.

In the new place, we spent hours without bumping into each other. Sometimes I had to go and find where she was and stay next to Claire for a few minutes, sitting on the ground beside the raised beds perhaps, just because that had been the normal distance between us for so long. But was it too much to take on? Suddenly we had moved from a simple life to one of endless projects. The barns needed repairing, the house had to be rewired and plastered, there were goats to look after, chicken sheds to fix, residency papers, language classes, the list went on and on.

Every morning, we stretched our limbs in the huge bed, ready to witness the rhythms of the day: the cows and sheep that passed outside the window; the saints' days and festivals that studded the year like jewels; or the neighbours who turned up at the door with fruit, vegetables and strange requests. In those first months, our western gaze saw only the colour and the light and we were far too glassy-eyed to see the grit and the shadows. That all came later.

We had come with our eyes firmly on the future and for most of that first year we did not see the layers of ruins all around us. It took time to feel the melancholic atmosphere of the place. In those early months we dealt with work and freedom and the beauty of the late summer as the walnuts fell and the grapes ripened and our first ever batch of wine began to ferment.

The pair of houses we bought seemed to go together like twins. In the 1920s, two brothers had inherited the land and built each one side by side. They faced a park filled with mature trees, Pine, Spruce, Birch and Horse Chestnut. It was our very own arboretum. Baba Petya told us that the park used to have rose beds and benches and a fountain in the middle but these days the entrance was blocked up with wire. Unlike the neglected buildings and the rotting fence posts, the trees in the park were majestic and immoveable. In those trees, I saw the future that someone else had imagined 50 years before, when they had planted the young saplings.

The park defined the *mahala*, our neighbourhood because all the houses that were spread around it considered themselves to be neighbours, almost part of a collective. So that was where we had to start, to get to know everyone and to show ourselves to be people who wanted to do the right thing, to be good immigrants. After weeks of intensive living, looking inwards to each other we knew we had to start reaching out.

3

Dead Neighbours

Pokriv lived on the other side of the park and every morning, he came out to see us as we waited for the shepherd with our goats. Each day he taught me a new word and soon I knew the basics. Goat: *koza*; sheep: *ovtse*; dog: *kuche*; sleep: *spi*; rest: *pochivka*; and beer: *bira*. 'What else do you need to know?' he asked. Then he added *pochinal*, which meant resting or dead and *umrieli*, the dead.

His belly did not bulge through his T-shirt like other Bulgarian men. He lived alone in a tidy house with an outside tap and a frame for the grapes, he had made himself from rickety poles. At the back there was a field of *lutserna*, alfalfa, but he had no animals any more so he gave the harvest to dancing Stefan as winter feed for his sheep. Four times a year they would come together to cut it with scythes, sweeping through the green stalks like silent machines. He had a craggy face with dark eyes and a thin beaky nose. The other British people in the village called him 'fingers' because he had lost the two middle digits of his left hand. In the bar, they talked about the way he could skip over the roof tiles in his socks. I never met his family and thought nothing of them until much later, when we were looking for his next of kin.

Pokriv could dance up and down ladders with a chainsaw which is why he was given that nickname, because *pokriv* is Bulgarian for roof. After a few days we showed him the barn. It was dilapidated and dangerous but he was sure he could fix it. On the first day of work, he left his shoes on the ground, taught me the word *stalba* for ladder then balanced on the top rung in stocking feet, leaning out with the deadly machine to cut the beams. I was sure that something bad was going to happen. Either he would cut off his arm or the whole structure would fall down on top of him, but it never did. After ten days the barn looked as good as new. It was our first renovation project.

He must have told the neighbours that we owned a brand-new chainsaw, because it popped into Baba Petya's head minutes after she found her husband dead on his chair in the living room. Petya was Simona's mum and Simona was our closest neighbour. Even though we saw her every day on the corner, at that early stage we had no idea whether we would ever get to know her properly as a friend. Then the old man died and we did not need to think about it anymore. In the village everyone used the Turkish word *komshi* for neighbour which seemed to indicate a golden connection. Neighbours weren't always close but when they were, when your neighbour referred to you as *komshi*, then you may as well have been family.

Baba Petya and Simona banged on the door at 4.30 am. Not the garden gate this time but the front door. I woke up and went with them to Petya's house where we dragged the dead man upstairs so they could arrange him on the bed in the guest room. In the morning they were going to announce his death and wait for neighbours to come and see his face for the last time. When the three of us carried him up the stairs, my forearms under his armpits, the body still smelt like a living man, sweaty, boozey, with a hint of almonds. After that, I went back to bed and tried to sleep but I was so fired up with the shock of handling a corpse that all I could do was stare blankly at the ceiling. By 11 am I was back there with the chainsaw to help Pokriv cut planks to cover the grave. Once we had finished, Petya made some space in the kitchen crowded with mourners. She cried and sobbed and held our hands and sat us both down like children, giving us each a shot of *rakia*, with a boiled sweet, as restoratives. I was not sure whether to sip it or swallow it down in one so I watched Pokriv. He drank so slowly that I wondered whether he was actually drinking at all. The *rakia* tasted like a strong fruity whiskey but without the caramel flavour of a single malt. When the spirit dissolved, I was left with the heady tones high up in the roof of my mouth and at the back of the tongue, places that were not accustomed to taste.

I tried not to look at the dead man in the open coffin but I had no choice. He had a long face like a horse and I could see several other people in the room with similar profiles. The family noses drooped down those faces like melting wax. Simona's nose was not like that because this man was not her father. Her real dad died when she was a baby but that was a story for another day.

By the time I was ready to go, Claire had come to join us and we both left the house together, still crowded 'like a wake at home,' she said. Petya introduced us as her new English neighbours, *Anglichani*, and if Claire, who is from Derry, objected to being called English she didn't say anything. Perhaps that was because it felt like we were now part of the neighbourhood, the *mahala*, the six or so houses that faced the park. The only empty one was on the corner and it was there, we waited every day with the goats.

The village shepherd was forever trying to get more money but every time he raised the monthly fee, there was a boycott. The old women kept their goats at home and watched from inside the garden, to see if he would change his mind. In the end he gave up the job completely and went back to collecting scrap metal. Daily common grazing over centuries had given life to the pastures that surrounded the village. The number of household beasts was dwindling fast and now, for the first time in years, the grasslands were re-wilding. The blackthorn scrub and plum bushes grew back all across the grounds simply because there were no longer enough animals to keep the undergrowth in check.

Once the shepherd had given it up, we took the goats out to graze by ourselves, at least until we found someone else. We walked them to the abandoned gardens below the pump station. These five houses were beyond repair and foxes made homes in the cool cellars with the wide stone steps. Eventually one of the English immigrants, *Anglichani* bought them all and broke up the ruins for building stone and roof tiles. The goats loved the old trees in the gardens and never tired of munching the fallen plums or the acacia flowers. I couldn't help but think about the lost families, so I made up stories to pass the time and to fill the spaces of memory that hung amongst the creepers and the dust.

Some days we would go down the steep lane where the ruts flowed with water after the rains, or along the road past Petar's house. Between here and the monument, there were eight fallow plots, none of them ploughed in spite of the good soil. Forty years ago, this whole swathe would have been filled with people digging between the rows of glossy maize plants, horses and carts waiting to take away the harvest of yellow cobs. I was there one day with the goats, imagining the scene, daydreaming under those trees, watching the goats as the ground shivered in the heat, squinting at the colour of the sun. Then all of a sudden, a man lifted himself up from the grass. He couldn't see me but he had been sleeping in the middle of the overgrown fields amongst the memories and the dreams. It was Pokriv and for some reason I remembered what he had told me about the verb *pochivam*, and that in Bulgarian the words for resting and dying were the same.

It was a warm evening during our first full summer and for weeks, it never seemed to rain. Pokriv's *lutserna* had been gathered in and the field stalks were so dry that it looked like nothing would grow in that parched ground ever again. He was sitting in the first room with a glass of beer and a plate of *kebapche* and bread. It was the perfect end to a working day, no television, no family, no pets, just himself and his thoughts and his small luxuries. I envied him the simplicity of his life, being able to jump into bed as soon as it got dark. He had a few close friends, but I didn't realize who they were until later. He never attended the village festivals, and looking back, I think he deliberately avoided being around too many people.

23

By the time it came around for the next cutting, things had started to go wrong. When the shepherd told us that Pokriv was sleeping in the woods, I walked past his house and looked over the wall. There was a carpet of fallen apples under the tree, and the *lutserna* had already gone to seed. His long-handled scythe lay across the steps, the blade bursting with pimples of bright rust. But where was he and why had he stopped doing the normal things that made up his life?

I went home to find Pokriv standing outside our house. The old suitcase and trench coat made him look like a refugee from the Second World War. He asked if he could stay the night and as soon as we were inside, he went straight upstairs and put on pajamas. In the morning he ate his yoghurt and eggs, and if there had been a reason why he was scared to sleep in his own bed, he did not say. After that day we didn't see him again until weeks later, but by then something had happened to make him stop eating altogether.

Before he left the house that morning, I showed him the two porcelain vases that stood on the chest of drawers on the landing. They were made in the Meissen workshops in Germany, 300 years ago. I still check them to see how precious they are. My dad always said they were the most valuable things in our home, the hand-painted arcadian landscapes, the rosy pink-cheeked couples with delicate miniature faces. Dad knew how much I loved them, and I used to think of him sometimes. These days they remind me of Pokriv too, because on that morning he spent a long time studying them and it made me think that he was an outsider like me and that I was an outsider like him.

When I went to the post office Kaimet asked why she had not seen me for ages. My mind had been on other things beyond our little *mahala* and even beyond the village, thinking about my three sons in England. Maybe, part of the condition of being an immigrant is never being completely present in your new place. She told me that Baba Kuna, Pokriv's aunt had dropped her scratch card on the floor of the post office. Everyone in the queue watched her do it but they assumed it had already been scratched. Now she had gone home, they all encouraged me to follow her and return it so she could win the jackpot.

In Kuna's barn there was an old plank to stop the door opening. Pokriv was unloading boxes from the side of the road and piling them up by the door. He looked terribly thin. There were two bags of clothes and a plastic box containing salami, cucumber, margarine, coffee and a mobile phone. I studied it all as he went inside to talk to his aunt. She raised her voice to say she did not want him staying with her but I imagine that was before she realized how sick he was.

Kuna lived in one room, down a steep flight of stone steps but I never saw inside. The un-occupied bedrooms were on the first floor and full of cobwebs. The street dogs lived in the barn and that day I saw one of them hanged. It was dangling from a rope tied around its neck. She was sick of cleaning up the dog shit, she told me as she cut it down from a beam. I was so disturbed by that image that I forgot to give her the lottery ticket.

The following day Baba Kuna turned up at the door and it was my son Max's birthday because I remember the phone ringing and Alex his brother calling from Glastonbury. He had gone to the festival car park to meet his other brother Josh and had seen all the missed calls and then rang me to say he had no idea where Max was but he would tell him happy birthday from me.

'Pops where are you?' he said. Of course, he knew where I was; in another time zone on the other side of Europe.

Baba Kuna was waiting on the bench outside. She watched Petar in a heavy coat, all cleaned up that day because his cousin had come from Gagovo and taken him away for a shave and a change of clothes. She tapped the side of her head and said quietly, '*toi ne e dobre*,' he is not ok.' Then she took me back to Pokriv's house and I noticed that someone had moved the scythe and put it against the wall. I saw the *lutserna* still uncut and the apples brown and sunk into the ground. 'He's back in the house,' she said to me at the gate, 'the nephew.'

The first room smelt of nothing at all, with no sound but the second room smelt like rotting teeth. There was a shape in the bed, under the clothes. A small man. He moved when he heard the door open and the feet on the rug. We stood by the open door just inside the bedroom and Baba Kuna reached out her arm to stop me going any closer. She just wanted to show me. Then she jerked her head to the side to motion us out of there and fussed around the door as if she were locking it.

Pokriv had not eaten for ten days.

'He refuses everything I give him,' she said with her eyes open wide. She looked desolate.

The next day we tried to give Pokriv some goat milk because Kuna said he would not take the shop-bought stuff. It dribbled down his stubbly chin and she gasped when he swallowed a mouthful. I heard her take a breath and hold it. She knew that taking milk was like taking food but that was the only time he drank any. The next day he just pursed his lips and shook his head. Then he got out of bed slowly and walked like a dead man to the outside tap and there he lay down beside the concrete sink to gather his strength before he reached up, turned on the tap and let the water rush into his open mouth.

Kuna had piled the sideboard in the bedroom with food; A loaf of bread, a jar of peaches, a block of white sheep's cheese *sirene*, Shumensko beer and two pork *kebapche*. She was hoping he might change his mind in the middle of the night. Instead, it was like she had furnished his tomb. The room began to smell strangely sweet. I stood by the window watching him, his pelvic bone stuck up beneath the blanket. The leaves of the Mulberry tree flashed like gold in the sunlight. The only sound was the beetles chewing on the old wood like munching silkworms. If I could have stopped time altogether then his body might have ceased its wasting but as long as I could hear the beetles, the minutes passed.

Could I have tried harder? When I called the ambulance, the medic tested his heart and blood pressure and told me that it was not an emergency. 'The man needs a psychiatrist,' he said. We whispered at each other urgently but the medic raised his hands in frustration and left. I watched him taking plums from the trees as he walked down the lane. Afterwards, at home, dripping butter from a bacon sandwich onto the pages of a book, I wondered if I would ever open it again at that same place to see the buttery stains and remember the taste of that afternoon. By then of course, I would know exactly what would have happened to him.

Kuna's final attempt was the strangest. I took her in the car to Opaka to see the wise woman, the *hodja*. She had been there once before when her mother was alive but she had forgotten where the house was, so we asked around in the main street and eventually looked over the wall into a yard where a lanky boy was plucking a chicken. Kuna fiddled with a bundle in her hands. The *hodja* appeared in the doorway and we saw how tiny she was. She wore the baggy Turkish trousers and headscarf and carried a book. It had a worn cover with no writing and the pages were incredibly thin like a bible. I think it must have been the Koran. She told Kuna that her sister's boy had suffered a difficult birth and that later he had fallen and hurt his leg. Kuna did not seem surprised. Then the *hodja* gave her a folded piece of paper with writing on it and told her to sew it inside his pillow without his knowledge. Kuna handed over 5 leva and the *hodja* was not pleased when she held out her hand for change. The old woman just flattened the note against the book. All the way back to the village, Kuna complained about having to pay such a sum.

Two years passed and I did not say anything about this to Carla, who had recently retired from her teaching job in Spain. When she told me how she was going to turn the ground floor of Pokriv's house into an open living space with French windows onto the garden, I never said I had been there before. I did not want to spoil her retirement so I didn't even mention it when I saw the scrap of paper on the floor. Perhaps Kuna had stuffed it between the floorboards. The scrawling black script in the *hodja's* hand looked like the tendrils of a vine reaching out across the page. There was another piece of paper too, which had the name of a doctor written in Cyrillic and a phone number. Both had been pressed together and then misplaced but as I looked, they unfurled and unfolded. The black lettering scorched through the paper and burned it away, losing its meaning completely. I couldn't see any flames as it burnt, as if the sun was shining directly on it, and soon the paper had turned to ash and there was only the slightest hint of smoke so I tried to inhale it to make it disappear and for Carla not to notice.

I only ever went back there once again after that. Carla had invited us for dinner. We sat around the big table, the oiled beams above us, glowing in the low IKEA lights, recently installed. We smelt the wood polish and the scented candles and the pork roast. Some of Pokriv's old farm tools, a scythe and hayfork, had been lacquered and hung on the wall. But all I could see was the sideboard in his bedroom laden with the food he never ate and the sight of him lying there on the floor when we found him dead, his legs stretched out towards us from the bed, like stiff wooden boards.

4

Krainik

I was on my way to see the man they called Krainik. His house was at the end of the village and I wanted to ask him for a favour. So there I was, one Spring morning, delighted to be alive, walking across the bridge as the wind bothered the leaves in the poplar trees high above my head. The tree trunks were a metre across and the bark, grey and coarsely indented like old elephant skin. This was where the goats walked every day. They crossed the bridge in single file and then spread out to follow the shepherd and wander through the open pastures. I saw something red in the woodland. A flash of lettering. New signs were hammered into the ground and on each one, somebody had daubed two words in Cyrillic, частен имот, *chasten imot*. It meant private property.

I knew all about it from England. As a kid, growing up in East Yorkshire, everywhere had been private; the woods, the fields, the pastures, all of it forbidden for us to access.

The English countryside is closed to the public after all. If ever I ventured off the road, I would see 'No Entry' plastered across field gates but here in Bulgaria, I had found none of that paranoid closure. In my new home, two hours from the Black Sea, nobody will challenge you walking across a field or straying through the woods to pick mushrooms. The countryside around the village is open and accessible, its ownership loose and uncertain. Maybe that was why I had taken to the place. So where had these signs come from? Who had declared the strip of woodland by the stream to be private property and why?

I rang the bell and waited by the gate. Krainik did not say anything but stood in the doorway looking up at me. Once inside, he said, 'You are tall.' And then, pointing up to the top of the high wall, he added, 'just like my new neighbour. He is also from England.' The old man led me past racks of tools to the garden where we stood together in front of his pride and joy, the polytunnels that filled his vegetable plot. They called him Krainik because the word literally meant limb or extremity and that described the fact that he lived on the edge of the village but I would like to think it was also because he was a bit of an outsider. He had short legs and, in each tunnel, there was a step ladder so he could reach up to open the windows in the roof. He was proud of the fact he had made the polytunnels from reclaimed doors and water pipes. Later on, as we said goodbye at the gate, he ignored the CCTV cameras on his neighbour's wall and pointed up instead at his flag saying, 'This is Bulgaria,' and shrugged, 'but there is England.'

The next morning, Krainik turned up at 9 am with a khaki tool bag slung across his shoulder. He accepted a small coffee and asked to see the site, the place where we were thinking of having a polytunnel. When I took him to the garden, he nodded his head firmly to signify the negative. A strong negative. He closed his eyes and wagged his finger from side to side to reinforce the point. He did not like the site at all. It was too close to the walnut tree. It faced the wrong way and there was some problem with the soil. We sat down together and said nothing for a few minutes. Both of us stared ahead. It was awkward but eventually I turned and told him emphatically that there was no other place. We had to build the polytunnel there. Reluctantly he grunted agreement and wrote down a list. Handwritten Cyrillic is much harder to read than the printed version so it was impossible for me to decipher. He read each item out slowly and I copied it down in clear printed letters.

'You write like a five-year-old.' He said, 'My little grandson is better.'

The list included 10 m of flexible wire, 10 m of iron rods and a huge sheet of thick plastic for the cover. When I asked him about the steel water pipes for the main structural frames he smiled again and made a gesture with his hand. I assumed he meant something like, 'I've got it covered. Don't worry about that yet,' so I didn't.

Before he walked off, back down the lane to the poplar trees I asked about payment and he pretended not to hear me, just carried on walking and waving his hand in the air. I agonized over whether it was better to hand over cash at the end of the job or just accept the gift of his time. Did he really intend to do the work for free? As things turned out, he already had a plan.

It was Krainik's new English neighbour who had put up the signs. He did not want anyone going in the woodland by the stream because he could see it from his sitting room window. In restricting access to his newly bought land, he was following familiar English tropes of privacy and entitlement that go back 300 years. In the eighteenth century through Enclosure, the British Parliament helped landowners to close footpaths and fence off common pastures, but here in Bulgaria enclosure had never happened like that even after collectivization, so the shared rights of access and grazing were still in order. I could feel the difference as I roamed the fields and woods. That was why the private property signs seemed so out of place. Krainik took no notice anyway. The previous owner had always allowed him to graze his sheep among the trees so as far as he was concerned the signs changed nothing and he simply ignored them. But still it bothered me.

I half expected that he might not come back but a few days later Krainik turned up again at the house. He had come to negotiate payment, only his proposal had nothing at all to do with money. Instead, he asked for a favour. I heard a voice in English behind him, 'Who's got my bag?' but anything else was drowned out by the Toyota pick-up, revving loudly in the street. Krainik said quickly that he wanted someone to look after his nephew and without giving us much chance to say no, he hopped back into the truck leaving Atso standing on the dusty road. Within seconds we were shaking hands with the lanky young guy who told us he had hitch-hiked all the way from Austria to see his long-lost uncle. Atso handed over a bar of Dutch chocolate, which he had carefully nursed through two lifts from Vienna to Sofia. The chocolate had melted when he left it on the dashboard of the truck. He tried to explain things,

'Krainik's house is minute and small and I don't know him. He gets up well early and snores all night. There is no way I can sleep there. You take volunteers, right? I'm not into spading or forking much but I am super good at cuisine and anything to do with food. Is it ok to stay?'

Of course, we said yes.

He spoke his own eccentric form of English and within five minutes of stepping through the door, he insisted on cooking some of his uncle's tomatoes. After an hour we were sitting down to a fresh pasta sauce. He dug down into the bottom of his bag and pulled out a sweaty wedge of cheese, Italian parmesan from a Budapest deli. He seemed well prepared for anything.

'What else do you have in there?' Claire asked and he emptied out the entire bag onto the settee. He held up the leather backpack and said,

'This is my house and these are my worldly belongings,' and reached over for a glass of wine.

Malaysian, on his mother's side, and Bulgarian on his father's, Atso had been travelling for a year with no money. He was testing the theory that you could survive entirely on the kindness of strangers. All he had in his pocket were a few Turkish coins given to him by a lorry driver. He spoke not a word of Bulgarian, even less than us.

Atso was learning to live like a wild man so all the next day, he watched the goats carefully as they tore into the undergrowth, sniffing the leaves and then folding them into their mouths. Later on, he told us over lunch that the goats did not often eat grass. They preferred leaves growing at head height and they would lift their front legs and reach up, stretching their necks. Sweet Acacia was their number one favourite. Atso picked some of the leaves and stuffed them in a bag to make a salad with plums and blue cheese.

I just need to tune into their mindset.' He said, 'These goats are great survivors.'

As we talked, we were sitting by one of the old springs watching the goats drink in a line. He told me that his wanderings had taken him all over Europe,

'In France it was a waste of time,' he said. *'La chasse*! The hunters! I nearly got shot in the leg by those guys.'

'England would be worse,' I said and wondered what would happen to him walking around the Yorkshire Wolds trying to live on the verges like the Roma travelers with their horses, camping on the parish boundary outside Dalton. The East Yorkshire Roma were one of the last groups living in the old-style caravans because in Beverley they had a machine for steam-bending the ash timbers, left over from the days of ship-building on Beverley Beck. My mind dwelt on far-off memories then jumped forward to the freedom of life in the van and I remembered the feeling of waking up in a new place with a sweet pang of loss.

A few days after Atso's arrival, the water pipes for the polytunnel arrived. They were lying in a pile under the walnut tree, all of them neatly bent to shape like the gable end of a house. I had no idea where they had come from and I didn't ask. Under orders from Ivan, we hammered one metre lengths of rebar into the ground and then slotted the open end of each water pipe over the rods so the frames stood up straight. Now it looked more like a structure. Then we joined the pipe frames together at the top and tied the whole thing down with guy ropes. Ivan worked at ground level, fastening each rope to a stick of rebar then hammering the metal poles at an angle into the soil. In my former life, working on archaeological digs, we used these same iron rods as grid pegs. We would cover each one with an empty beer can for safety because if you fell on the metal spike, it would do serious damage to your leg. I made a mental note to do something like mark the pegs with spray paint but I never did it and that was my first big mistake.

'Now the hard part starts,' Krainik's son said to us. 'All that digging is going to kill you. Too much clay. You will need to add sand. Lots of it.'

Atso soon became restless so after a few days he went off on a wander.

'Apples are all my body needs,' were his last words as he walked off with a full backpack to sort out some visa documents in Ruse. When we saw him again it was two weeks later. He walked into the yard with his arms full of broken wood.

'How are the goats man?' He said, and dumped what was left of the splintered private property signs on the kindling pile.

'What's with all this wood?' I asked him. 'You pulled up those signs?'

'Jesus I am super angry about that moron. I know what that means you know, *chasten imot*, private property. For fuck's sake. I have learned some other stuff too. It's like the words are already formed,' and he tapped the side of his head. 'My family history.'

'Do you want a beer or something?' I asked.

'Coffee will do. They only have instant down at Krainik's. Three-in-one. Coffee granules, sugar and milk powder. It tastes like shit.'

For two weeks, he had been living like a hermit, walking through forests in the Rusenski Lom National Park, following the rivers Lom and Cherni Lom, from Ruse all the way back home to the Popovo hills. The river cut through the limestone massif in a wild secluded canyon, hidden from the arable plains above by steep cliffs. Today it is a nature reserve but in the Middle Ages this river gorge was crammed with monasteries. All the way down there were holes in the rock-face, small caves for the hermits, puncturing the cliffs like the nests of bee-eaters. The caves were fashioned for orthodox monks, the Hesychasts, who in their meditation strove to see the white light of the Transfiguration. The monastery at Ivanovo had been set up by the Bulgarian Tsars in the thirteenth century and it was royal money that had paid for the beautiful paintings on the walls of the rock-cut churches. One of them showed the Last Supper, from the same view as Leonardo da Vinci's painting but here, executed 150 years earlier, by a painter from the Tarnovo school. By the time da Vinci painted his own version Bulgarian lands were already under Ottoman control and, like Constantinopolis and Salonika, could never be part of the Renaissance. In spite of all this, the paintings are still as vivid as they ever were, preserved in the dark chillage of the cave.

'That stream flows into the Danube man. I followed it back like a home boy.'

Back in the fourteenth century, the monks from *Ivanovski Manastir* the monastery near Ivanovo, lived on little else but fruit and water. One of the frescoes shows a bearded man squatting inside a cave and Atso had stopped shaving so after two weeks he was starting to look a bit like him. But it was also the name, Ivanovo that he liked because it was his family name.

'When I was sleeping in the woods, Ana Ivanova brought me coffee and pancakes,' he said, 'That Nova Brasilia is undrinkable but I sipped it so she would not be insulted. This is Italian, ok?'

'Lavazza. So, you pulled the signs up?'

'Yeah man. Someone had to. The English Empire is finished. Those days are over. I've seen that guy driving up and down in his Range Rover.'

'It's probably all on camera,' I said.

'He was watching me from inside the compound. I saw him.'

And then he winked at me, pulled out his grandfather's pipe and filled it with tobacco. He sat there puffing away, lost in thought.

'Krainik has gotten used to the idea that I am like a tramp. He told me that the more I smoke the less food I need.'

Then he added, 'Anyway you shouldn't worry about stealing the Englishman's water pipes because my uncle told me that they had been lying around in the field for years anyway, so in a way they don't really belong to his neighbour at all. You shouldn't feel bad.'

I didn't feel bad. I knew Atso was right. Private property can be fluid.

We worked hard in the polytunnel, digging, planting, sowing seeds, but however much we reached out for the future, something kept coming back. Death was part of the atmosphere of the village. It was sewn into the fabric of each house, built into every mud brick and ploughed into the soil of the gardens.

Our new polytunnel was close to the garden fence and its doorway faced towards another vegetable field. The two women who lived there were mother and daughter and both were intrigued by our garden activities. Gabriela was 78 years old and walked with a lurching stoop as if she were examining something on the road. Her mouth was usually set in a grimace but when she sat down for a cup of tea or when Claire gave her a small gift she would smile like a goddess. She wore home-made clothes that were perfectly sewn with tiny stitches and rough seams. She had never let go of the old ways, the outlook of her grandparents before the modern age arrived with its machines, fertilisers and cash wages. Her earliest memory was about loss. Her father left for America when she was seven, just before the Second World War and she had never seen him again. She held that sadness in her face most of the time, looking down at the ground so as not to see the world, her skin like soft leather. Perhaps because of that early parting, she always worried whenever we went away, that Claire and I might never be coming back.

As new immigrants, we were keen to do the right thing and Gabriela felt the same. For her, this was to show the new neighbours from the west a good welcome but she was shy. She turned up one morning with her long-handled hoe, *motika*, and announced that she was going to help us prepare the beds. Maybe she would get a polytunnel too, if it was worth the effort. At the end of the morning's work, she asked if she could put some of her seedlings in there.

'It is a big space,' she told us, 'Just for two.'

As we gathered up the tools and walked away, something made us look back as if we didn't really want to leave the work behind. Krasimira appeared on the other side of the fence and maybe she distracted us because we did not see the vicious metal pole, the rebar sticking out of the ground, still uncovered, still un-painted. Gabriela tripped on the rope and fell, her full weight landing on the spike, gashing her leg on the steel edge, jagged from the cut I had made a few days earlier with a new Bosch angle grinder.

As soon as Krasimira heard her mother cry out she rushed onto the street and ran in through the gate, for once ignoring the etiquette of knocking and waiting. The blood was soaking into the ground so much that the soil changed colour and so did her face. Baba Gabriela looked sad like a wounded animal.

'Your car.' Krasimira said, 'Popovo hospital.'

As we carried her out, Gabriela tried to shake us off but every time she put her foot down it failed to connect with the ground. The pain was yet to arrive. She was floating. When the feeling came back, once the adrenalin had slowed down, hurtling around those old veins, she was already in the car. That was when she began to sob. The front tyre was flat so once we had her in the passenger seat, I had to inflate it furiously with a footpump, my eyes wide, heart beating and the blood throbbing inside my head. Claire and Krasimira leant over from the back seat tending to her crying face, tears on the weathered skin, as the leg itself continued to seep blood into the makeshift bandages.

A week after the accident, the signs in the woodland disappeared for good but then a fence went up. Krainik ignored that too and went inside through a gap which mysteriously opened up one night. It didn't matter anyway, because the new mansion was never finished and the English family went away, back to their place in France. The Range Rover no longer flew up and down the road.

The old arrangements were restored. Often, we saw Krainik selling tomatoes at the market and he would show us pictures on his phone, of smiling Atso in far flung corners of the world looking skinny and healthy. He always had the pipe in his mouth. The boy who could live on fresh air but when it came to coffee, had a taste for the good shit.

'My brother's boy,' Krainik said, 'he came all that way.'

As for Gabriela, we visited her in bed every day as she convalesced at home. Thanks to her sweet forgiving nature the accident did not destroy the relationship between us and if anything, made it stronger. But her time was up. Just as quickly as she recovered, she fell again in her own garden and this time, she died in the back of an ambulance on the way to Popovo hospital.

5

Back to the Land

It seemed like they had forgotten the drill so I banged the stick hard on the tarmac behind them. The sun shone on the dark green spikes of new grass as the great herd hurried down the lane towards us. Violeta and Simona had decided I should be the one to handle the money so I gave the coins to the new shepherd, Hrasim. He nodded at me and shouted old Turkish words at the goats who had wandered off into the hedge. This was our new arrangement. We paid him 7 leva, 3.50 euro a month for every goat which was good value considering he walked them through the pastures all day long. He did not even take a day off on Friday for the market.

'Kris. *Utre kakvo shte pravish?* What are you doing tomorrow?' Violeta said in a piercing voice as the herd disappeared beyond the poplar trees,

'Can you look after them until Hrasim comes? We need to be at the hall for nine.'

Simona tried to say something in protest but her friend stood firm,

'Chris will manage things fine *Monche*. You should be there.'

They were going to the *Sabranie*, the annual meeting of the village co-operative, which they still knew by its old name, the *TKZS*. It stood for *Trudovo Kooperativno Zemedelsko Stopanstvo*, or Workers Co-operative Agricultural Holding, the name given to all the collective farms which had lasted from 1947 to 1990. After the end of Communism in Bulgaria, in most cases the *TKZS* were disbanded and the land returned piece by piece to the former owners but in our remote corner, far away from Sofia, they regarded the old regime more fondly. Here, after 10 November 1989, they did not want to get rid of the *TKZS* at all so the villagers chose instead to become shareholders in a new venture, the *Corporatsia*, which was eventually established in 1992.

The *Corporatsia* bakery was on the ground floor and everyone with shares had a book of vouchers to exchange for the soft white loaves. They gave out the bread from a hatch in the cool hallway where the air always smelt of delicious baking. The faux marble steps led up to the Post Office and on the sixth day of the month the corridor was full of people waiting for their pensions. As I stood there, wondering what to do, the crowd shuffled up on the long seat. Someone patted the space beside them and a row of friendly eyes encouraged me to sit down. On the wall, the faces of 92 men and six women stared out from behind the glass of a large picture frame. The title read 'The Founders of the *TKZS* "Victory" of Podgoritsa Village, 14 November 1949'.

Calling them 'Founders' as if they had given up their land willingly was rewriting history, turning them all into socialist heroes because, in truth the land had been taken from them without consent. It was a shock to see the picture above the pension queue hanging there like a monument. It seemed out of place in 2013 but then it struck me that it also said a lot about how the village was dealing with the memory of the former regime, 20 years after its end. This picture had not been taken down and smashed like in some other villages because here, the *Corporatsia* did not represent the replacement of the old *TKZS* at all, but a kind of re-branding, a simple fork in the road.

Many looked back warmly on the old days. There was a water fountain to the memory of a local party man decorated with a large red star. The star, sunk into the concrete, had faded over time and lost its colour but one night in 2012 somebody came out with a brush and paint and re-daubed it with a fresh coat of red. These days, it gets a new lick every couple of years. When foreigners see it, they nudge each other and roll their eyes as if it shouldn't be mentioned and, despite Bulgarian membership of both EU and NATO, nobody in the village is inclined to contradict the quiet statement made. They just live with it, walking past the red star every morning on their way to get the bread. Just like always.

If there was another place on the planet less likely to have its own red star, it was my Gran's village in East Yorkshire. Lund was twice voted 'Best Kept Village in England' and every year, on the open gardens weekend, visitors could wander round the rose beds and manicured lawns and breathe in the sweet aroma of climbing honeysuckle. Villages in England are neat and tidy as if the countryside has been cleansed. In Dalton, where I grew up, there were never any animals in the street. Instead, the cows and sheep were scattered in picturesque order across the fields, safe behind hedges and gates. Everywhere looked like a Constable painting. Podgoritsa was not like that. It was peppered with rubbish, broken cars, dogs, goats, plastic bottles and piles of metal. It was edgy. It did not resemble the postcard image of a village at all and that is why we liked it.

In Podgoritsa, they kept goats, sheep, rabbits, chickens, pigs and cows because they provided milk, eggs and meat. They had cats to catch the mice and dogs on chains to scare away the foxes. As far back as Ottoman times the village had been famous for its sheep and for the embroidered garments woven from local wool on household looms. The houses clustered around the *polyani*, which were small pastures where the flocks used to gather before leaving for the grazing grounds. Animals were at the heart of the calendar of festivals too. St George's Day, *Gergiovden* on 6 May was the holiday for sheep farmers with *Todorovden* for horses, 50 days before Easter. The folk songs reminded us to eat chickens on *Petrovden* and fish on *Nikulden*. When people in Popovo or Razgrad wanted a beast for slaughter they drove to Podgoritsa to buy a lamb for the Muslim feast of *Koch Bayram* or a goat kid for Easter. At Christmas, some families spent the day pitching in, to slaughter a pig in the yard.

The traditional skills of subsistence had disappeared from the villages we knew in England, and it was difficult to live in the UK without finding yourself beholden to industrial farming. By shopping in Tesco, we were giving our money to billionaires, every week buying meat and vegetables driven across the country in trucks, whose useless packaging went to landfill. We knew that British land was expensive and the regulations made a nonsense of any sustainable plans to produce food from backyard pigs. So instead, we had planned our escape by reading books for inspiration, ready to leave when the time came. Dreaming. Plotting. Hoping.

Helen and Scott Nearing were American socialists who, in 1932 had left their jobs as teachers to retreat to a plot of land in the US state of Vermont, where they built a house and grew their own food. Their book, *The Good Life* has been a bible for the 'back to the landers' since the 1960s. They lived and worked by a strict regime and I have no idea how they did it because being self-sufficient on only four hour's work a day would require iron discipline. We soon found out that once those four hours were over, there was always more to do. We had no intention of replacing one dogmatic structure with another, so we worked each day for as many hours as we could. In the first few years, the energy that came with our new way of living meant that we never stopped.

If the Nearings' book had told us what was possible, it was *Self Sufficiency* by an Englishman John Seymour that showed us how to go about it. In the book, he describes a total agrarian system on a beautifully small scale with perfect permaculture solutions on every page. The pig for example is a useful beast because she eats all your waste food and turns it into manure. She can plough the garden plot and transform fallen apples into pork. Seymour preferred full-on off grid self-sufficiency but you could follow any of his practical activities without going the whole way. The godfather of smallholdings would not have approved when we ran out of preserved tomatoes in March, but we were not slaves to his philosophy either. We took a lot of ideas from these books but both of us felt kind of irreverent towards gurus so we did not copy their systems wholesale. Once in Bulgaria we still had mains water and electricity and we often bought food in the supermarket. As we got ready to leave the UK, it was the simple dream of growing our own roast dinners that had driven us on. Living in the truck with our pot belly stove and solar panel, we felt like pioneers, listening to folk songs about the freedom of the road as we chugged slowly down the slick Euro motorways.

Where did it come from, this urge for a simple life? Was it anti-modern? Were we trying to make something new or just retrieving folkways that had been lost in the west? In Podgoritsa, every household compound had a vegetable garden, fruit trees and grape vines as well as sheds for animals, hay drying lofts and a barn. When we arrived in 2010 there were still enough people producing their own cheese, wine and sausages at home. Most of the things we read about in Seymour's book were there, knowledge handed down for generations and it did not take long to realise that Yavor had been right. We had found the perfect place to go back to the land.

But things were changing in the Bulgarian village. From as early as 1960, people had been moving to work in the cities but it was not until the 1990s that the young generation began to emigrate *en masse* to the west. Most of the families with kids moved to Popovo or beyond and by 2000, both schools had closed. Grandparents stayed behind but when they died, the houses were left empty. Neglect. Some of them were used as gardens. Reuse. Some fell down. Abandonment. Others were bought by foreigners like ourselves. Rebirth. Many of the British people who moved here were looking for a simple life. A few wanted to reconnect with nature but most were just trying to escape.

The western ideal for sustainable living is a reaction against industrial farming, consumerism and pollution. Even though it borrows practical skills from the past it is a radical position focused on the future of the planet. The ways of life in the Bulgarian village were coming from somewhere much more conservative. People had lived like this for centuries and for most Bulgarians, doing small scale farming was not radical at all. It was simply considered to be, 'what the old people did'.

Here was the tension. We had set our hearts on a fresh, alternative way of life but here we were trying to make it work in a traditional rural society. How was it going to succeed for Claire and I, when we had chosen this remote corner of a country, which was one of the least progressive in Europe. Don't get me wrong, I love this place, the people and the landscape, the music and the food, but to a nosey historian like myself, there is a way of thinking here which guides attitudes, a way of thinking that is fixated on death and the injustices of the past.

After her mother died, Krasimira went through the usual mourning period, wearing black and staying in the house but even after the 40 days of public grief, she never returned to her old routines. The bright purple colouring in her hair faded away to grey and whenever I saw her, she held my hands more tightly than before and bowed her head and told me how much she missed her sweet mum.

When she said, 'All of this is too much for one person,' I was not sure if she was referring to the garden work or something else. She moved like a shadow. We watched her walk past the house to the bins and Claire said,

'She is even beginning to look like Gabriela.'

When her mum had become anxious about being left alone, Krasimira used to treat it as a joke. Now it came as a shock to be alone herself and I think she took on some of her mother's fears as if she was literally stepping into Gabriela's shoes. And maybe she was just preparing herself for the next one because no sooner had she put up the *nekrolog* to mark the 90 days since her mother's passing, she had to make room on that sorrowful door for another.

That evening when the goats came back, Hrasim was at the front and he walked forward to ask who had died, for he had heard the death bell ringing out in the field. None of us knew exactly who it was for. They considered all the possible candidates and as I listened, I saw that the browsing goats had shaped the lower branches of the mulberry tree like topiary. It reminded me of Hampton Court maze. Sitting below the green canopy, Violeta said,

'Kris! Do you need *echemik? Echemik! ECHEMIK*!!' Her voice grew louder with every word, as if I were deaf or something. She was asking about barley.

'Todor will take you,' she added, 'get your sacks ready, he'll be here in an hour.'

Having heard so much about the *TKZS*, the time had come to see it for myself. Every shareholder was a descendent of one of the 92 faces on that picture on the wall by the Post Office. They received an annual dividend as grain, oil, bread or bales of *lutserna*. The barley was only supposed to be for those with shares but Violeta said I could put the sacks down under Simona's name.

Every now and again the exhaust pipe on Todor's van backfired loudly. Bang! The two of us jumped in our uncomfortable seats. My plan was to collect 100 kg of barley so I could mix it with maize to make forage for the pigs. We parked the van by a hangar-like building close to the flat scales. The mound of golden barley looked like millions of grains of sand. It was busy in there, people moving about with metal buckets and shovels. Simona had measured out perfect lengths of soft fabric for her son to tie the neck of the bags and Todor held them carefully in his left hand. I walked into the shed with my own sacks and bailer twine and looked around for someone who could show me what to do. The barley grains, piled up in heaps seemed to glow with a golden halo of fine dust.

I watched as Margarita (Milk and Honey) hold the bags open while Pesho her husband shovelled up the grain. Margarita once told me not to feed my own goat with fruit when they were out with the others because it looked too much like flaunting your favouritism. This collective ideal must have been drummed into her at school. Then there was Dobri the Mullet in his pork pie hat. Vanya told him to put out his cigarette as he moved between the bags, tying them up and heaving them over to the scales. Cruyff was there too, his black trousers tucked into socks to stop the fleas jumping up. A pig slaughter man, his work was like theatre. When the rifle clapped and the pig fell silently, he would turn towards me in slow motion with a slight raise of the chin as he cocked the gun to pop out the smoking cartridge. Sometimes he posed for photographs with the rifle to show off the tattoos on his back, a leopard reaching up to the talons of an eagle that hovered between his shoulder blades.

The older men shouted to each other across the crowd. A long diatribe about houses ended with the words,

'Todor Zhivkov! He gave us our pensions! Now his bodyguard is taking them away!'

The Prime Minister at the time, Boyko Borisov was an ex-wrestler who in the 1990s had taken up the job as the former dictator's bodyguard. Everyone got stuck in to help the others and it felt like a kind of solidarity. Todor held the bags open this time and I shovelled in the barley. Vanya made the measurements and wrote down entries in a ledger. When I reached for the pen, she said it would go under Simona's name, that way the price was cheaper. She winked and smiled quickly before going back to the scales. Then she remembered something and her face went dark and she looked at me to check my expression. 'How is Krasimira?' she said and I assumed she was referring to the continuing grief for her departed mum.

As we pulled up outside the house and unloaded the bags of barley, I could see there was something wrong. A black car was parked outside Krasimira's house and there were people standing in the street. Then I remembered the bell from the day before and my stomach felt empty. Inside the house, Krasimira was sitting on the bed surrounded by the neighbours from the park. It seemed like a wake but, as well as the usual hushed respect, there was a kind of desperate anger. Like some terrible injustice had occurred. There was no box and no body. Outside in the garden her daughter Nadia was speaking loudly on the phone and she cupped her hand over the handset and told me quickly what had happened. Krasimira's brother Bogdan had died. He was a body guard and his car had crashed near Sarajevo. The Bosnian authorities were not going to give up the body without an investigation and so nobody knew when they could bring him home for the burial. It had all the sadness of a sudden death without any possibility of the consolation offered by the usual ceremonies. It was a limbo and everyone around the park was stunned.

The days between the death and the funeral stretched on. Every morning we went round for news but there was none. All the neighbours were out discussing events, except Simona who was lurking in her own yard looking up at the commotion down the street.

Once they did return the body, Krasimira was desperate. She had her brother back in the house at last but it was only going to be for one day. Dobri the mayor told her that the lid must stay shut. Violeta had a prime seat in the room with the closed box. That was always her place at funerals. She was there to welcome people and to hand out sweets and to delicately fill in the silences with small talk. How Violeta could stay there for so long, I do not know but there were plenty of other women prepared to do the same. The room was pretty full.

It was lunch time when I went round to pay my respects and Krasimira was trying to eat something quietly with Nadia downstairs in the kitchen. She nodded at me with a mouthful of *banitsa* but her mum just stared ahead. Upstairs in the room, Violeta thought that this was a good time to tell me that Krasimira was not the only one around here who had suffered from loss so she beckoned me over. She crossed her legs and began to tell me the stories, half whispering to show some respect and not to disturb Bogdan during the last few hours in his family home. When I could not follow the detail of her tales, I listened to the sound of the words, and through their rise and fall, suddenly felt the dead man's presence in the room. I was struck by my sudden awareness; the place, the time, the people, my journey and theirs, captured in phrases and words and the sound of Violeta's intimate direct speaking, hushed and urgent in my ear. I could almost see him through the sides of the coffin.

Violeta broke the spell as she crossed her legs again and my thoughts wandered off to our guest house on the other side of the wall and how, two years before when the place was empty, I had sneaked into the garden to pick the blackberries that grew up through the box hedge. Behind the shuttered windows the rooms had lain under a spell. I tiptoed through them, amazed to see the posters of the Soviet space programme and the radio-set with cities like Tallin, Kiev and Prague inscribed on the dial. Years before, this had been the childhood home of a man who left the village to become a diplomat in Moscow. His books on agronomy and physics were stacked up against the wall in one of the bedrooms as if someone had just taken away the shelves. Wild hops shrouded the garden gate. A bright Peony bloomed on, in a burst of deep red.

Violeta broke off her story because someone else had come in. This woman settled herself, with arms folded. I knew her. She was so tall she rarely sat down, as if it were too difficult to bring her lanky frame from an upright position and too uncomfortable for her to balance long limbs and torso together on a chair.

They were talking about another empty house, the one on the corner where we waited for the goats because somebody wanted to buy it and nobody could remember who had the documents.

'That deaf one lived there after her husband died and then I think she went off to Sofia,' the tall woman said.

'Well, you should remember best, of course you should. You only live over there,' said Violeta.

'I used to live there. Not these days. I am in Popovo with my son, as you know.'

Violeta and Simona and all the women of their age were children of Communism. Born in the late 1940s, they had lived most of their lives under the same regime but this did not mean they believed in it. These women did not look for comfort by dwelling on the old days. In fact, they had no interest in politics at all. What really defined them was their ability to survive through turning plants and animals into food. They made remedies for tomato blight from sheep's milk and rubbed pig fat on the goat's udders when they were cut by thorns. Simona knew that white mulberries were good for the heart because her grandfather had told her when she was a kid.

After some time, the tall woman extracted herself painfully from the chair, stretched her arms and legs and walked out. I had lost track of the minutes completely by then and was beginning to feel comfortable, almost part of the furniture at this awkward event. When I left it was dark. Nadia saw me to the door and called me 'brother' for the first time and that was something that made me shiver.

The day following the *Sabranie* was warm. As a freshening wind dried the wet ground for the first time in months, it felt like change was in the air. All three of us had offered to look after the goats that day and in the end we all stayed and watched them picking around the hedgerow for the tiny plums. We were happy to bask in the beginning of summer. Then we heard Hrasim's voice and the faint tinkle of little bells that sounded like a mirage.

At Bogdan's wake, Violeta had told me that the funeral of a child is a very different thing to that of an adult. She said that her own son had drowned when he was ten and after that sad event, her husband had never recovered from the grief. He died five years later himself. These families experienced death like falling dominoes. Simona too had lost her husband at a young age. This was one of the few times she ever mentioned him. She complained about the wall he had built,

'Look at it. One day that wall will fall on me. And then he'll be sorry,' she said.

'Then you can tell him yourself,' Violeta said.

Violeta was drawn to funerals. Her son's had been a visceral experience, lighting up her senses like electric wires with a fizz and tingle that made her feel alive. For Simona it was different. Her experience with death had caused her to retreat.

Simona went into the house and brought out a plate covered with a patterned serviette,

'For you and Claire. In case you have any guests,' she said and handed over a mound of small cakes.

'I can make you some walnut bread,' Claire said, 'in return.'

'Well, I may have to start doing it myself soon. The *TKZS* are going to close the oven.'

'So, what will you do for bread?' Claire asked.

'Probably just buy it from the shop.'

'Like everyone else?'

'Yes exactly. Like everyone else,' Simona said.

The next day, Violeta and Simona were holding flowers and they told me they had been to say goodbye to the breadmaker on his last day of work. Simona thrust a carrier bag at me and said,

'Smell that, Chris. Still warm. I got the last one.'

'But not for long. It'll soon be stale,' Violeta said.

'So, we'd better enjoy it. Tomorrow we'll have to pay,' said Simona.

'Sliced up in the plastic packets. How much does it cost anyway?' Violeta said as if she were not used to money.

'Or maybe Claire can teach us?' said Simona.

'I've got no time for making bread,' Violeta said as she opened her carrier bag and brought her face down to it. Closing her eyes, she inhaled. Then she laughed and turned to Simona,

'Did you see the baker's face when you kissed him?'

'Ha ha! On the lips.' Said Simona.

6

Myths

When Wally the dog was lost, we searched his favourite places and called his name for days on end, before we realised that he had actually gone away to die. The dog had a habit of always being around but suddenly he was no longer there, as if he had slipped away in a puff of smoke. We soon got a new one, Belcho but for years Wally lived on. In the summer garden, as we gossiped over endless evening meals, we remembered his exploits. The fireflies flashed and flickered in the dark and the tales melted into the night as our memories took root in the clay that absorbed him. There, they blended with the local ones, the real *Kapantsi* legends so that the ground became stuffed with stories.

This was a *Kapantsi* village and the local legends assured us that the first Bulgarian Khan to cross the Danube in the seventh century, came here. At the end of a long folk exodus, Asparukh picked up a handful of earth, held it to his nose and declared it to be the most fertile soil he had ever sniffed. According to the village tales, Asparukh and his people were free to stay because there was nobody else here. The legends claim it to be unoccupied land but historical accounts suggest the opposite. Annals preserved in Byzantine archives tell us without any doubt, that the Bulgars were just another wave of immigrants. People had in fact been crossing the porous frontiers of the Roman Empire ever since the third century and Asparukh and his band must have come face to face with a mixed local population. This included recently arrived Slavs from the north, Greek speaking Christians known by everyone as Romans and the people whose ancestors had been here before anyone else, the Thracians. There may even have been a few residual Celts left over from earlier incursions.

Like all the wandering folk before us, we were just another couple of nomads who had crossed the Danube to become farmers. As a young community, we even had our own myths. The first British couple in Podgoritsa, Darren and Janine, had come to the village in 2008 to sell property on Ebay. They were real pioneers. They took part in a TV documentary and were married on screen in full *Kapantsi* costume. For the rest of us who came after, this became our origin myth. But there was more than one version to their story.

There were rumours doing the rounds that the fairytale had a bitter ending when Janine took their daughter and went off to France, leaving Darren alone in the village. But what we remembered was the way that he cured his own bacon and distilled *rakia* from wild plums. These details did not feature in the stories we heard from other people, of how Darren followed his wife westwards in a rage to try and reunite the family. We had stayed with them for a month as volunteers and, in our story, Janine taught us how to milk a goat and walk the animals around the old gardens, bringing back branches to hang on the wire fences around the stalls. This young couple had shown us that our dream of a smallholding project was viable, and their inspiration had been enough to encourage us to stay.

Darren and Janine made a lasting mark on the community but they only stayed for five years. Bulgaria has always been the kind of place that people pass through. In fact, English visitors had been coming and going, staying for a time and then moving on for over a century. Some even wrote it down.

Patrick Leigh Fermor is best known for a journey he made at the age of 18 when, in the winter of 1934, he set out to walk from Holland to Istanbul. The first two books of his epic trip take the reader as far as Romania but the third one, *The Broken Road* describes the time he spent in Bulgaria in 1935. He writes about the lingering flavours of the Ottoman Empire in the halva slices and baklava. In the old town of Plovdiv, he stayed with a Greek speaking family and in Ruse, devoured German newspapers, ferried on Danube barges downstream from Vienna.

In 1935 there were already a few English people living in Bulgaria but if it weren't for Leigh Fermor's account, we would not know them. In Kazanluk, Fermor introduces us to Barnaby Crane who had come to the town to help mechanise the local textile industry. Over dinner the two men talked about horse-drawn trams in Manchester. Crane had made a life for himself and Fermor doubts, out loud on the page, whether his host would ever see Lancashire again. Once the evening is over and the paragraph closes, this man is completely lost to history. When Bulgaria entered the war six years later Crane would have found himself on the wrong side, with an enemy passport. Did he return to England or stay put? We will never know what became of Barnaby Crane.

After Kazanluk our young narrator crossed the Shipka Balkan and on the other side of the mountain, he was taken to meet a sick Englishwoman in Gabrovo. Betty was still in her early twenties when Fermor spent the evening talking to her from his seat on the threshold, keeping his distance as she was suffering from Scarlet Fever. Her husband was away in Sofia and Leigh Fermor describes a poignant scene, the sick room cluttered with lace and pearls, her copy of Black Beauty on the bookshelves and a framed picture of York Minster on the dressing table. It is easy to forget how far away she would have felt from home but like Barnaby Crane, Betty too slips out of sight as PLF waves goodbye in the twilight and is led off through the darkening streets of the town to his lodgings.

The scale of immigration to Bulgaria since 2007, is remarkable considering that the country was never one of the places like Spain or Greece, where British people went to find sunshine or antiquity. The unconditional welcome we received when we arrived was due to the very small number of British and Irish citizens who had already played a part in the national story. It properly began when William Gladstone supported the Bulgarian cause against the Turks in 1876. There are schools and streets named after him to this day but it was not just Gladstone we had to thank. There are other streets in Sofia named after Englishmen too.

Steven Runciman first came to this country in the early 1920s, a good ten years before Patrick Leigh Fermor wandered through the Rila mountains in his hobnail boots. A cherished passage in both biographies is their first meeting in a Sofia hotel in 1935. Runciman was in town for the Byzantine Congress and the young Leigh Fermor walked in off the street and introduced himself to the scholars. The two of them became friends for life, sharing an interest in Byzantine History and a certain classical perspective on learning that defined elite scholarship before the Second World War.

Runciman had learned Russian and Bulgarian so he could read medieval documents for research. He is famous for writing the definitive history of the Crusades as well as many other books including the classic and celebrated work, *The Fall of Constantinople*. His debut, published when he was only 25, was called *The First Bulgarian Empire*. He later earned a street name dedication in Sofia because this book had introduced the country's history to the English-speaking world. In the 1970s, he was one of the very few western academics to be invited to Sofia through his association with the culture minister, Lyudmilla Zhivkova. The two of them shared an active interest in the occult.

For my first few years in Bulgaria, I knew nothing of the English women and men who had been here before me. I was too busy planting tomatoes and milking goats. Today, people like Mercia MacDermot, Runciman and Frank Thompson feel almost like relatives, as if I am writing about my half-remembered uncles and aunts. They have become a kind of yardstick for my own feelings of belonging, as a foreigner in this country. I feel a kinship with them.

In families there is a kind of collective memory, a social museum where stories are shared, but not everything is on display and a lot of things are forgotten. In my own family, our best-known ancestor is Edwin Fenton, the ultimate patriarch, my great great grandfather who died in 1930. We know him because he set up the family shipping business in Hull in the late nineteenth century. I even have a lock of his hair in an envelope that somebody snipped off his dead body. We know a lot about Edwin but it is much harder to remember the names of his brothers, sisters and cousins. As it is in families, so it seems to be with countries. Certain people are chosen to be memorialized and it is they that become the emblems of the nation.

The old truck that carried us here, watched our comings and goings from the side of the road and eventually became part of the landscape itself. The wheels slumped down into the ground and Claire planted marigolds in front of the flat tyres. We dreamed of starting the engine again and taking off, back on the road to Greece but we never did it. The interior of the van was like a museum to our journey and one day, looking for mosquito coils, I found a lighter from Melk Abbey in Austria, where we had stopped all those years before. It took me back to a time when everything about Bulgaria was in front of us, an unknown future. The thought of that was almost like time travel and I had to sit down on the soft cushion and let the nostalgia wash over me.

In the cupboard with the coils, there were two small treasures, a pair of books given to us by Yavor on our last night in the Pyrenees. One was the story of Vasil Levski, by Mercia MacDermot and the other, the poems of Hristo

Botev in English translation. Inside each book he had placed a photograph of a town square, one for Botev's Kalofer and the other for Levski's Karlovo. They were like postcards from a former life, almost intended as invitations.

Vasil Levski and Hristo Botev. In Bulgaria, the faces of these two men are everywhere. You see them on coffee mugs, T-shirts and exercise books, even stenciled on the back windows of jeeps or painted up as murals on the walls of secondary schools. They are the symbols of the nation's history and their portraits hang in every public building. Bulgarian national identity began to emerge in the monasteries in the early nineteenth century and within decades, these feelings had turned into an uprising against Ottoman rule. This is where we find the martyrs, Levski and Botev. Levski was a revolutionary organizer until he was caught by the Turks and hanged in Sofia in 1873. Botev, a poet who led an armed band in the 1876 rising, hijacked a steamship on the Danube before he too was killed. Of the two, Botev became the main symbol of national memory under Communism but these days Levski is better loved. He is sometimes called the Apostle of Freedom and that was the title of Mercia MacDermot's book.

Like immoveable statues, Bulgarian history has rested on these two patriarchs ever since the independence of 1878. Their narrative of martyrdom is so strong, it has cancelled out other versions. The Ottoman centuries from 1388 to 1878 are seen as nothing but oppression and the martyrs Levski and Botev as saviours who gave up their lives to free the Bulgarian people from this slavery. That was the story.

In 2015, whilst checking into a guest house in Sofia, the receptionist described to me, without invitation, how Bulgaria had lost its history. With bitterness in her voice, almost like grief, she told me how her people had missed out on being part of the Renaissance, the Enlightenment and even the Industrial Revolution because they had been de-coupled from western Europe by the Ottoman Turks. She was reflecting an entire national consciousness. This idea of loss is so strong it turns any other telling into heresy.

At Stevrek near Antonovo there is a stone bridge deep in the forest. The eco trail follows an old pack horse route across the Balkan Mountains. The Ottomans built bridges like this all over their empire. I parked the car and looked around for directions to the old bridge then went over to talk to two men bent over the engine of a van with the bonnet up. '*Rimskia most?*' One of them said and pointed the way up a track beside the main road. The signs on the trail called the monument a 'Roman bridge.' I knew this bridge was not Roman and so to see it written like that was a shock. The bridge was actually built in the sixteenth century but to call it an Ottoman bridge on public signs and brochures would be to undermine the narrative of slavery. Nobody can admit that the 500 years of Ottoman control may have actually brought useful things like trade, transport innovation and architecture. Instead, everyone portrays the bridges as Roman. Let's not forget that Rome, centuries earlier, had also been an imperial power, but that period has none of the loaded memory of oppression and cruelty that is attached to the Ottoman Empire.

What we remember from our own childhood is filtered through the stories our parents told us. The things they wanted us to remember. Sometimes, as adults we forget who we are because we have always relied on our parents'' narratives. When other memories come back to us, they can appear almost like dreams, like the moment in Marcel Proust's novel *Swann's Way* where a childhood memory is triggered when the narrator drinks tea with a Madeleine cake. For me at Stevrek, stumbling across this 'Roman' bridge and then finding out it was Ottoman was like seeing the truth uncovered and I wanted to shout it from the rooftops. The revelation felt like a lost memory in the same way that, when a long forgotten scene comes back to you, its power over you is the truth that it holds. But this had happened to me before.

Driving away from England in 2010, to reach the ferry terminal at King George Dock in Hull, Claire and I drove along the A63. Wally looked out of the back window as ever. Beneath the new road, were the graves of an Iron Age cemetery where we had worked as archaeologists uncovering the crumbling skeletons. But apart from its ancient history, that place had another special meaning for me. We were close to the Humber Estuary and one day after work, I walked up into the woods high above the site to look down over the water. I found fresh puff balls under the beech leaves.

I had spent my childhood only 30 miles inland from here and I had no real memory of ever being so close to the water. We had always seemed to look north to the market towns of Driffield and Malton. From the hilltop lookout, I could see the massive diggers on the roadworks and the broad silvery strip beyond, the old muddy river that was more like a sea. As I gazed out over the view wondering how to cook the puff balls, something triggered a lost memory. But it was not a smell or a flavour that caused the mental slip. For me it was the place.

The Humber Estuary. The shipping lane. In a flash it all came back. I suddenly remembered that I had stood in that same spot years before. My dad was there, my mum too and all the family watching a troupe dancing around a Maypole, all of us laughing because our dog was barking and running round and round the circle of people. They all got into the car but I did not want to leave the place so I ran back for one last look to see the sun reflected on the water. I did not care about them all shouting for me to get in the car not even when dad blew the horn and I guess I was smiling as I turned back. I was eight years old just weeks before I left home for boarding school. That memory lay dormant for 35 years. The vision of those distant drifting channels where tidal salt brine mixed with fresh river water had stayed hidden all those years. When I saw them again, they were powerful enough to propel me into the future.

Six years after the day I found the puff balls, we all sailed away. Claire, myself and Wally left the country by sea from the port of Hull, passing slowly by the coastline of East Yorkshire, which had been my home for most of my 40 years. The ferry rounded Spurn Point and headed across the North Sea. We arrived the next morning in Rotterdam to set off like the 18-year-old Patrick Leigh Fermor, diagonally across the continent, to the far corner of Europe.

7

Simona and the Goths

I met Dimo for the first time on the steps to the *chitalishte*, the village hall. Everyone said he was looking for new members to join the band. He was smoking a cigarette before the concert.

'I am not very good,' I told him, 'Just a beginner'. He shook his head for yes like a smiling Buddha.

'*Ucha oshte az*. I am still learning.' I said, 'I cannot even read music.' His eyes lit up.

'I have never played in front of a crowd.' He took a drag and smiled again. 'Except Wally and Claire and my old teacher.'

'You had a violin teacher? Bravo.' He clapped his hands silently.

The next day at the music school in Popovo, I played an Irish jig on the fiddle as a kind of audition. Dimo said, 'if you can play that, then you can play anything,' but I suspected this was not true. Straight afterwards, he conjured a tune of his own on the accordion and it sounded more complicated than anything I had ever heard. With unexpected pauses and trills and a strange broken rhythm, I was struggling to tap my foot.

'You'll be playing that perfectly in a month,' he said, 'only slower.'

'The festival is next week.' His colleague added.

'You can join in with the easy bit.' Dimo said and winked at me. I was in the village band or to give its full name, the *Selo Podgoritsa Kapantsi Orkestar*.

At that first festival I scratched away hoping nobody would hear as I hit one note in three and thankfully stayed back from the microphone, shared with Pesho's *gadulka* and Ivo's clarinet. A photo of the band from that day hangs on the wall of the library in the *chitalishte*. It was a typical summer scene, all of us with hot red faces and big smiles. There is me standing at the back in my *Kapantsi* outfit, in red kumberbund and white embroidered shirt. It was the beginning of a three-year stint in the band. Every weekend we piled into the minibus and set off. Playing such unfamiliar tunes in public was terrifying and it required a great deal of practice to learn the songs by ear but I loved the excitement of waiting to go on, all of us huddled together with our instruments next to a bright stage that could have been anywhere in Romania, North Macedonia or any Bulgarian town.

Pesho the *gadulka* player was always totally relaxed. An old man in his 70s, he winked at me and tapped the hip flask on his belt passing it round the men in the *orkestar*, each one sipping draughts from the bottle as if it were a drinking horn. Dimo watched over us like a football coach trying to get the musicians in the right order for walking on and sharing the microphones. The others were always sipping *rakia* but I had to keep sober otherwise my fingers instantly forgot where to move or which notes came next. It didn't matter to Dimo what happened backstage as long as we all had straight faces when we walked on. He told us that we should never smile, even after the performance, 'because it looks like complacency'.

Simona's cousin Iva sang in the choir and the two women spoke on the phone every day so Simona knew about upcoming concerts before I did. When we went on tour Simona would look after our goats but I rarely had the chance to return the favour because she never went anywhere. She liked to stay inside the house or the garden and dreaded the thought of ever having to go to Popovo.

I saw her twice a day as we waited for the shepherd in the morning or for the goats to come back in the late afternoon. One such afternoon we were outside her house, standing around by the pink roses. If the goats stood on the low wall to nibble the flowers, Simona said that it didn't matter. She would even let them eat the pears that dangled down from the big tree. Her rubber shoes glistened above the mud of the lane and we edged back against the wall to let the cows go past.

'You know he had sheep once,' Violeta said in a loud voice so Petar would hear. 'You had sheep didn't you Petri? *Oftse*! When your mum was alive.'

Petar said nothing.

'Off you go Petri. Go away. You smell.'
Violeta pressed her lips together and Petar, red in the face with his black pin-prick eyes, reached down to stroke Belcho but the dog squirmed away. Then Violeta followed her goats along the lane towards the bridge and home.

Simona pulled up a sock over the tracksuit bottoms with the triple adidas stripe and slipped her tiny foot back into the rubber shoe.

'She is worried about getting bitten by a tick,' said Iva, 'Claire, doesn't she look like an old woman in that scarf? Like a village woman.'

'She is a village woman,' said Claire.

The four of us laughed and Simona stood next to Claire and they held hands like sisters. Simona looked young but she was already well into her sixties.

'I could not live here without you,' she said tidying away the hair from Claire's eyes. 'These ones,' she waved her hand shyly to the houses around the park, 'they are not really my people.'

'Chris, don't be so embarrassed by women talking,' Iva said as I made a move to follow the goats up the road and then she came over and held onto my hand,

'There's no choir rehearsal this week so I am taking *Monche* to Draganovo to see my mum,' she announced.

'Overnight?' Claire asked and Simona nodded, 'Do you want us to feed the dogs?'

'And the rest of the zoo.' Iva said. Simona kept quiet.

Her yard was full of chickens and the house overflowed with cats who scattered whenever the dogs lurched towards the gate stretching the chains with a rattle and a snap. The countless rabbits were in five separate cages. Some had tiny ones wriggling in nests of fur.

She had left out old bread for the dogs with a pot of cold meat stock and while she was away, I ladled it once a day over the stale slices. Simona's house was worlds away from the homes of my childhood but there was something about being alone in there that took me back to my gran's place in

East Yorkshire. The boot rack and the coat hooks felt the same and the tiny alcove by the door where she left the key. The inside smell was similar too; savoury cooking and a whiff of perfume and bleach.

The summer music festivals were often tied up with historical themes. The Roman town at Razgrad used to have the Latin name *Abritus* and even though the construction of the pharmaceutical factory had destroyed some of the buried archaeology, much of the ancient city survived. We performed there one evening as they re-enacted the famous battle when Cniva's Gothic armies had defeated the Roman legions in 251 AD. It was the first time a Roman Emperor had ever been killed in battle and we watched Decius die over and over again as the soldiers performed for the crowds on the hour throughout the day. The site was only 40 km from the Danube frontier and in the third century, thousands of Goths had gathered on the northern side and streamed over to threaten the citizens. At the evening concert at least half of our audience were dressed in togas and by the end of it, the Goths in red cloaks were dancing with the Romans in white. Iva took a photo of the *orkestar* with one of the Gothic warriors, a huge man from Stara Zagora dressed in nothing but a bear skin. She said she wanted to show Simona because her cousin knew all about the Goths. It was strange to think that Simona would be interested in these nomadic people whose sights had always been fixed on the distant horizon. The very opposite of a home bird like her.

Simona was soft and humanist and she cast her love around through a pair of gentle dark eyes. She was critical of unkind behaviour and avoided funerals. It was not death she was scared of so much as that period of limbo, just before the burial. The one or two days. Because it was during that time, the day after her husband's death that her uncle had also died. It was these two men she had been closest to in her life, for she had never known her father. *Nekrolozi* for the three of them had pride of place on the garden gate, declaring forever, her grief to the world. The interest in the Goths though, was nothing to do with them, instead it came from another one altogether. A man she had once been in love with. Her first.

She said it might help encourage my sick chicken to eat again so a day or two after Simona got back, we walked up to the top spring by the *Corporatsia* compound to find the herb. Standing on the ridge, the whole village was spread out in front of us on both sides of the valley.

'It used to grow by the Roman walls. Look, they are making a car park for the tourists.' she said, 'There will be nothing left of that herb now.'

We looked down on the ruins of *Kovachevsko Kale* which had been a fortified station on the Roman road to Nikopolis ad Istrum and its massive stone towers were being rebuilt with a European grant. She told me that in the summer when the sunflowers came out, it would be a beautiful sea of yellow all the way down to the road.

'I cannot even see my house,' she said smiling and picking at the grasses. The sky was completely clear and we gazed at the smoky tail of an aeroplane.

'Where do you think it is going? To Sofia?' she asked.

'Could be Germany or Belgium,' I said.

'Or even Italy?' she said and craned her neck upwards.

'I used to have a friend who said he would take me to Ravenna. He told me about the cities of Italy and how the Goths walked across the frozen Danube. Then they rode their horses all the way to Rome.'

She was sitting on the ground, with her legs stretched.

'So did you ever go?'

'No of course not Chris.'

'And what about your friend? Why was he so keen on the Goths?'

'I think that was because they had been free to travel wherever they pleased because of course, back then we were not. Look at me. I've said too much.'

'And did he go to Italy?'

'He lived there yes and then he died. I always thought I would go first.'

Then she quickly got up and brushed the dried grass from her trousers and said that she must go home because her mother, Baba Petya would be wondering where she was. The sky above was milky blue and full of grace and possibility but I walked back to the village alone as the Golden Orioles darted above me in the trees singing their hearts out like crazy flutes.

In the markets round here during the fifth century AD people would not have been speaking Bulgarian. They would have used Greek words, Latin words and Thracian words but also maybe a few Germanic ones brought here by people whom historians call Goths. These Goths had settled in their thousands just inside the Roman frontier. From this corner of the empire, they travelled south and west where they made history. Alaric took a force of horseback warriors and sacked Rome itself in 410 AD. After that the great Gothic King Theoderic ruled over the whole of Italy. The Goths had made their mark on Spain and Medieval France but they started their journey to imperial power here, in the fortified stations and towns along the Danube frontier.

Places that are now called Svishtov and Silistra.

We were having tea with Simona in Baba Petya's tiny kitchen when I asked if she wanted to come to Silistra for the day just so we could see the Danube. Simona looked at her mother who tightened her lips and said nothing but we all knew what she meant.

'The tomatoes will not grow by themselves,' Simona said.

'When was the last time you went to Silistra?' I said,

'I know that but I am worried about leaving Tara after the dog bite,' Tara was the oldest of her goats, the matriarch of her small herd.

She came to the door to see us out, 'If my husband were still alive, we could all go to the Danube together.'

A few days later as I walked back from the goats, Iva was sitting outside her house on the bench, waiting for her husband Dobri,

'Nothing to do until then Chris so come and sit with me and have a drink,' she said.

'I wanted to ask you about Simona's friend. The one who went to Italy,' I ventured.

She gulped, 'She told you about him?'

'I didn't ask. She just said it.'

Iva drank down her *rakia*.

'Years ago, they used to meet by the *mogila*. Before she was married.'

'The legend of Antola?'

'Exactly. For her, it is more than a legend.'

'So, what happened?'

'She was only 17 and everyone assumed they would get married. Unlike Princess Antola she had no father to censor her boyfriends but then Stefan announced he was going away to study in Rome. He wanted to be an archaeologist like you and eventually he got a job teaching at a university in Ravenna.'

'He walked out?'

'Not exactly. He gave her a choice to join him him but she decided she could not leave home. Krassi, a school friend was next in line. They were married pretty quickly after Stefan went. She was in pieces on the wedding day.'

'What became of him?'

'He died in May. The family sent her some things. A book I think.'

The next day I stood in front of Simona's gate and looked at her husband's face on the *nekrolog*. It was blurred to a smudge on the photocopied page. We were checking the goats for ticks before the shepherd came.

Violeta had a clear narrative on bugs and insects. Flies were a nuisance but harmless, ants were industrious and should be left alone, bees deserved respect for their co-operative spirit but mosquitoes, ticks and fleas were dangerous parasites that should be killed without mercy. She would drop the ticks on the hard surface of the road and squash them with a stone so you could see the dark blood ooze out of the sack.

'They will be sucking blood all day like vampires,' Violeta said as she came up, delighted that I might find one.

Simona was there too and she held the goat's head and I examined the skin around the udders and pulled off the young crawling ticks before they latched on. She had been weeding all day and her fingers were stained from the wet soil. As she flashed her dark eyes, I noticed how brown they were. You could see the colour, but only in a certain light, otherwise they seemed almost totally black.

'The rain has brought the weeds up,' she said and picked small blue fruits from her pocket and chewed them with her front teeth spitting out the pips to the side. Then she handed me an A4 envelope but said nothing, motioning with her eyes towards the house.

It was an article written in English and at the top of the page was the blue and yellow logo of the European Union. The title was, 'The Goths in Bulgaria: A view from Archaeology,' the text amended in pencil. The author was Dr. Stefan Kolarov, University of Ravenna.

The next day I tried to hand it back but she told me to keep it because she could not read English and anyway, she had a whole book to get through. Then she said,

'Are you and Claire free this weekend?'

'I think so, yes,'

'Keep Sunday free. We're going on a trip.'

Sunday came and Simona had been up since dawn. She was in her best clothes, the black leather coat and floral scarf as she silently waited for us on the bench. Without a word. Then we set off for Silistra on the Danube, the ancient Roman city where the Goths had held power.

When we got there, she handed us cheese pastries and doughnuts as we looked down over the water from the ruins of the Roman wall. She had made a whole picnic.

'The Goths even worshipped the river,' she said, reading from her book. 'You can see why can't you?'

The water may have been a barrier but it was also a way in for thousands of people to enter the imperial territory and discover a whole new continent.

'Do you think they crossed here? It does not look far to Romania,' Claire said.

'The Romans ferried them over in boats. Thousands of them, too many to count,' Simona said, 'according to this book.'

These were the words of Ammianus Marcellinus, written in the fifth century,

"Accordingly, having by the emperor's permission obtained the privilege of crossing the Danube and settling in parts of Thrace they (the Goths) were ferried over for some nights and days embarked by companies in boats, on rafts and in hollowed tree trunks."

The history books portrayed the Goths as barbarians and, under this narrative, the Danube at Silistra was nothing but the edge of an empire. And yet, the river had been the entry point for wave after wave of new people. The Goths were mercenaries who had ruled the frontier for two hundred years, then moved on to govern Italy. They were immigrants just like us and I thought to myself that I was no longer living in the far corner of Europe at all, but in the middle of something else. I was seeing the re-orientation of a place still being made because the frontier of one thing can also be the centre of another.

On our way home we had a surprise for Simona. The restaurant by Popovo Lake had re-opened. The tables looked over the water and she told us about her long shifts in the kitchen from 4 am to 10 pm. Decades before, almost in another life, she had worked in the state-run restaurant with her husband Krassi and catered for coach loads on their way to Varna. We ordered mackerel because Simona told us the Carp from the lake would taste muddy if the cooks did not go to the trouble of flushing out the silt.

'I have decided something,' she said, folding the napkin in front of her as if she had already finished, 'Iva has persuaded me. I am going to join the choir. Life goes by so fast. I want to learn to drive before it is too late. Krassi was always the one who did the driving.'

She rarely said her husband's name.

'Yulian says he will get me a car from Germany, a small one that runs on gas. Then next time I can take you both out and you can have a beer.'

Before we could say anything, the drinks arrived and the three of us clinked our glasses together and made sure we looked into each other's eyes. There were tears in hers.

8

No Borders

When we said we might open a guest house, everyone thought it was crazy. The property oozed golden charm but Podgoritsa was in none of the guidebooks. There were no mountains or seaside resorts anywhere near, so we had to persuade the foreign tourists to make a special trip, to see for themselves. And come they did.

The day always began with the goats. There were over a hundred beasts in the herd and watching them come down the hill from the Dolna Polyana along Gagarin street, with their bells tinkling was something very special. To share it with the visiting families reminded me how lucky I was to be witnessing the scene every day. Monny and Denny knew exactly what to do. Just at the right moment they peeled away from us and walked slowly into the mass of hooves, fleeces and horns. One of the visitors might make a joke about dropping the kids off at school and that would be the cue to head back to the house for breakfast.

All the produce came from the garden. There was goatmilk, yoghurt, cheese, bread, jam, eggs and bacon so the food miles were close to zero. We made everything ourselves and we did not sell any surplus so I think the guests appreciated the small scale of our operation because even for just a few days, it was all for them. That is what we did for six years. Was it only that long? Looking back, it seems more like 15. All those yoga retreats, airport runs, herb workshops, cheese-making sessions and historical tours.

For 20 years, I had been an archaeologist in Yorkshire and part of me missed the discovery of new places so I jumped at the chance to explore local sites and learn their secrets. The most obvious, like the old capitals at Pliska, Veliki Preslav and Veliko Tarnovo had their own gift shops and car parks but I preferred to take the guests to lesser-known ruins. They tended to have more mystery.

In former times this area had been filled with people from all over the ancient world because they passed through on trading routes between Europe and the Near East. They had come from Anatolia, Persia, the Mediterranean, North Africa, central Europe and every corner of the Balkans. The Arab geographer Muhammed Al-Idrisi was commissioned by the Norman crusader King Roger in the twelfth century to produce an atlas, the *Tabula Rogerina*, a series of maps of Europe and the Muslim world. The Idrisi map was compiled through interviews he had with merchants and it depicts some of the Bulgarian cities growing rich from trade. One of the places was called Missionis. It had markets and churches and its remains were only half an hour from Podgoritsa.

One morning in May, I showed them the Idrisi map and proposed a trip to Missionis as we sat around the breakfast table finishing off the yoghurt and honey. The couple from Australia and the young family from Leipzig all wanted to come so, as soon as the washing up was done, we set off in two cars. From the main road the signs led towards the hotel *Rai*, Paradise but we marched on instead to the small roadside restaurant with its neglected ecotrail that headed up into the hills. At first, we could hear the roar of trucks down below but once the trees grew back and the track dipped down, there was no sound at all. When the kids sang or shouted, their voices came back from the wooded hillsides, peppered with white plum blossom. They took photographs of the blooms but nothing could capture the smell which was so like perfume that the two German siblings looked around for something spilled.

There had been three churches in the original Byzantine city and they were marked by foundation walls but the gate towers stood to over 3 m in height. The footings of the former buildings were covered in plastic sheets and we had our tea in the archaeologists' wooden shelter, littered with broken walnut shells, sunflower seeds and cigarette butts like some midden. On the way back down, the path took us through pine trees and stands of coppiced hornbeam. We stopped under an oak to shelter from the rain and to swap stories. The German family told us about an old tortoise which their grandfather had smuggled back to the DDR following a 1970s holiday in Varna. Grandfather named the tortoise Krassio after a waiter in the hotel and he painted the name Красю in white Cyrillic letters on the shell. They told us that Krassio the tortoise had lived for many years in the family apartment in Leipzig, even outliving the grandfather himself who died in 1988. The tortoise had been an everyday connection to Bulgaria for them all and because of it, they had come to see the country for themselves.

We could see across the main road to the hotel and the swimming complex and the bright green façade of the spa which must have had 100 rooms in its heyday. At the archaeological site, there were fading signposts but no people at all and it felt like we had just discovered this place and wrestled it from the jungle ourselves. Missionis has never been claimed for any nationalist version of history. The narrative here, stretching back centuries, seems to suggest open borders, international trade and the mixing of people from all over the world.

After lunch we headed north past Targovishte and Razgrad to Isperih and the Thracian city of Helis, at least a thousand years older than Missionis. Its name is often mentioned in Greek sources but before the 1980s nobody knew the actual location. When Bulgarian archaeologists opened one of the huge mounds by the river Krapinets at Sboryanovo they found the finest stone Thracian tomb of all, Sveshtari. When they explored nearby ruins the archaeologists uncovered a walled city and most historians now regard this as the site of Helis. For 200 years in the third and fourth centuries BC it was a trade city bringing in goods over land from Greek colonies on the Black Sea and sending them on to the Danube for shipment to central Europe and the north. They abandoned the city after an earthquake but the river gorge lived on for centuries as a sacred spot, mysterious and holy to many different religions. The Romans called it Dausdava the 'City of the Wolves' and centuries later, in the sixteenth century a Muslim teacher and mystic known as Demir Baba chose it for his home. When he died, his followers buried him in a fine stone tomb which they built on top of Thracian sacrificial altars. His mausoleum survives intact to this day.

Demir Baba Tekke is a place of harmony and ancient faith where both Christians and Muslims come as pilgrims. The most magical surprises are the ribbons and offerings that they tie to trees all the way down the steps to the seven-sided tomb. The deep significance of this place is tangible and the mystery, felt by anyone who visits, is kept alive by the local population of Alevi who live in the surrounding villages. They are the guardians of the patron saint whom their ancestors buried 400 years ago and still today they keep his secrets. On the day of our visit, we finished off our sandwiches and cakes and joined local families who were camped out for the weekend to celebrate St. George's Day. They had come from the closest village and there was even a donkey tethered to one of the trees. One of the women had set up a fire and hot plate to make flat breads while her brother cooked lamb shish kebabs on the barbecue. The German kids wanted to stay the night. It reminded me of the free festivals we used to go to in Wales and made me wonder if there might be something missing from my new life, not religious belief so much as the social gatherings outdoors. The coming together of like minds in a field.

There was no escaping the fact that we were far from home. Miles from anywhere, we could feel the separation from the organic celebrations we used to attend; events like gigs, protests, film screenings and festivals. After four years learning to be a farmer it felt like it might be time to re-connect with the wider world. At least that is, the one we used to inhabit. Our initial plan was to screen a few films but once we got together with our friends, it soon developed into a music festival. For that we needed generators, sound systems, food stalls, bars, DJs and bands and a bit more time to prepare. The land was owned by someone we knew, but still we thought it best to inform the authorities. When we asked the police chief in Popovo he agreed with a shrug,

'Do what you like. It doesn't matter to me. It's not like you're criminals or something.'

On hot summer days in Bulgaria, I close the curtains to hide from the fierce blue sky. My summer diet is melancholy music and folk horror films. To escape the relentless heat, I bathe in nostalgia for northern Europe, walking down the wet streets in Autumn, spending the whole day in a library and long train journeys to nowhere. During one hot summer, a group of us planned the festival vibes. To the rebel guitar bands and bass DJs we added craft workshops, yoga, a book stall, nice food and some Bulgarian folk. We made it free. That way the good people would come. The free people.

We used a piece of land in the forest outside of Voditsa, where the mood was relaxed. That was the village where the other organisers lived. When the trucks of hippies and ravers trundled in from Germany and Romania, the people of Voditsa did not object, they just pointed the way up the lane. Some of the locals wanted to see the show for themselves and they came along and stood in front of the make shift stage to hear the acid jazz of the Purple Elephant or the teenage punks from Shumen, the Lefties. The Lefties were only 17 back in 2013 but have since become one of Bulgaria's biggest rock bands. Hip hop kids from Popovo had their own pancake stall. There was even a guy who had escaped from the 1990s rave scene, an English bloke called Acid Mick. He told us that he had left the UK with Spiral

Tribe in 1993 spreading the culture of free parties and techno to the world. One night he dressed like an eagle with a huge feathered head dress and I remember him coming over and shouting in my ear in the middle of the dance floor,

'Where's your fiddle man? Give us a tune later yeah, nice one.'

I had stopped playing in the band by then, but I asked Dimo if he would bring the *orkestar* to the festival and they all came down in two cars. The band members walked through the mud carrying instruments, the five of them still in their stage clothes; red and white embroidered shirts and clean black shoes. Dimo noticed how hard everyone was working. Some were carrying wood and lighting fires, some cooking, others feeding the horses or filling generators. It was a busy place and everyone was pulling together, for no profit except the party.

Dimo and the musicians played in a tent to about 20 people and the whole crowd were dancing by the end. The Bulgarians knew the steps and everyone else just followed along. Then we went outside to get some home made vodka and spinach *kyufteta* from Tomas and Lara's Polish stall and the musicians all said how it was like Bulgarian food but just a little different.

'A bit like the festival then?' I said,

'No, not like the festival at all. That is nothing at all like Bulgaria. It's like another world. It's more like an Ottoman Caravanserai,' said Pesho and the rest of them laughed.

Dimo came over and shook my hand in front of the crowd and I knew what that meant from a friend like him. He loved a party but he was still a conservative at heart and he knew that in all those concerts and tours with the village *orkestar*, I had been a fish out of water. Here, in this festival, I was closer to my own cultural home. The musicians stayed for the evening and while they watched the 1970s Bulgarian films like *Gospodin za edin den*, they left their instruments in a line along the inside of the tent and we covered them in plastic to protect them from the evening dew. For a few days the festival brought people together from all over Europe and the world, ignoring the formality of borders and blurring the grubby distinction between cultures. Was this a glimpse of the future or a flash back to the past? I was too busy filling generators with petrol to even think about it.

In those first five years we learned some lessons about how to be ourselves in a conservative place. We had to tread carefully, getting to know the people, respecting their values but never taking on those values ourselves.

I had often explained to people how we had found ourselves in rural Bulgaria but the question of why we had chosen somewhere so far away from the places we knew, had never really come up. It was my grand daughter Lily who asked first. She had come to the festival with her dad. On the last evening, Lily wanted to make sure the goats were okay and to say goodnight to Monny, her favourite and to read her a bedtime story. We left the festival behind for an hour and drove to Podgoritsa. She sat on the hay feeder on a soft bed of straw and read from a story book as I shone the light from my phone. I remember being struck by something she said, that it was best to have a little light on, as they would not settle down with the big one. As we walked quietly out of the shed the goats watched us, munching indifferently. She said,

'Why do you live so far away Grampops?'

'It's not that far.'

'It is,' she said.

'Think about how long it takes to go and see your nanny in Scotland.' I tried without much conviction, knowing she was right.

She was still thinking as I fastened the gate.

'Or daddy's friend in Spain,' I said.

'Yeah. That took ages. But Barcelona is kind of normal.'

'And here's not…,' I said.

I struggled to answer. Why here? After all, we could easily have stayed in France or even Portugal. Maybe there was more to this choice than simply leaving home to go to anywhere else but England. I did not know what to say. I hoped that next time she asked, I would have some kind of answer, even if it were not the true one. For that was still buried deep.

9

Cruyff

If ever I went away, I would come back to the same street corner where the village ends. That is where I will always remember them, waiting with the goats by the house with no documents. In a shaft of sunlight, Simona and Violeta. The two people around whom my village adventures were to spin like planets.

After ten years, I took my place beside those two, in that brilliant spot, for this was never going to be just about them. I had to bring my own memories, so that everything entwined as tales of immigration often do in places where foreigners come to live. Stories of belonging work both ways. I could never be one of them, because even though I was drawn to the light and antiquity of the south, I did not ever get used to the heat of the Bulgarian summer.

My dad loved wild moors and mountains, so for family holidays we always travelled north. First, we traced it on the map. Then, leaving early in the morning, we set off up the

A1 to Scotch Corner, seven of us in a Volvo Estate, past Glasgow and Loch Lomond, over a mountain called 'Rest and be Thankful' and then down to Loch Fyne and Inverary ending up on the west coast in Argyll. Mum and dad took us to remote lochs where we skimmed stones on the grey luminous water. Looking back on it now, I can see that they both upheld the gender roles expected in the 1970s. He did all the driving while she was perfectly poised in lipstick and headscarf and every lunch time, well prepared with hard boiled eggs and cooked chicken. After the picnic, hours later, we arrived at some cottage and were freed at last from the car to prise limpets off barnacled rocks. I spent the days looking for sea caves where I could watch the tide edge onto the wet gravel, dreaming of things hidden and searching all the crannies for crabs. I went back with books and cans of coke and found rock shelves where I could store bright pebbles. Until they called me back. Or shouted from the car.

Then one exceptional summer, instead of going north we went in the other direction, from Yorkshire to South Wales and it seemed like a tropical heaven. A few years later I fell in love with the south of France and after that, the north seemed too cold and too closed. Once I had felt the warm Mediterranean sun, the idea of the south was enough to open up all the possibilities of the rest of the world.

In Bulgaria, I would escape the heat of a Sunday afternoon by lying on the cool sofa listening to The Archers on Radio Four, trying to catch the sound of the rain pouring down in Ambridge. On the radio, the Bulgarians arrived in the west country to pick strawberries and Roy Tucker fell in love with Lexi from Stara Zagora. When they spoke about the churches of Sofia or when Lexi made *banitsa* with *sirene*, it was like a gap closing between the two places of

89

my life, confusing the cultural distance I had made as the essence of one place seeped into the other.

It was going to be *Koch Bayram*, the Muslim festival and when I said '*chestit praznik*' to him, Cruyff replied with something in Turkish. This made Hrasim look up. It was only 9 am and Cruyff stopped to tell us that he had already killed eight lambs for the feast. He had learned how to speak Turkish as a kid and there was not a hint of prejudice or judgement in his dealings with other people. That showed him to be an independent thinker.

'Too many in one day,' he said, and squeezed his hands together.

I asked him about doing one of our pigs and he showed me his bullet belt, touching the metal head of a cartridge and moving his finger tip around it in tiny circles,

'I can do it but not today. Now that's over, I'm going hunting,' he said.

After he had gone off in his battered Lada Niva, Violeta told me that Cruyff's real name was Stefan.

'He is a Christian. A Bulgarian. I knew his father. So why does he bother speaking Turkish?' she said, not really expecting me to answer.

The nickname, Cruyff was taken from the Dutch footballer Johan Cruyff who captained the Netherlands team that beat Bulgaria in the 1974 World Cup. In his younger days, our man looked just like him and in case we forgot the name, someone had engraved the word C R U Y F F on the blade of his butchering axe.

He was born in Krepcha where there was a mosque instead of a church. It was only 10 km away but in Krepcha the gardens were so small that they stacked winter wood on the pavements like the mountain villages of the Rhodopi.

Some of the older women could not even speak Bulgarian, only Turkish and for Cruyff, the Muslims of Krepcha and Opaka were his neighbours and friends. When he spoke Turkish in public, shouting the words across the village square in Podgoritsa, it made all the heads turn.

I saw the butchering axe for myself a few days after *Koch Bayram*, when he came to kill our pig. Taking the rifle from the back of the car he showed me his gun licence, laminated in clear plastic and stamped several times by officials from the Popovo Municipality, *Obshtina*. He laid the document on the table as if it were a job interview. Then he said something about Bulgaria being a serious country where you need all kinds of licences for different guns, not like in England where you can buy them in grocery shops and I thought that he must actually be thinking of the U.S. In any case that all seemed irrelevant when, minutes later the crack of the rifle shocked the garden and I turned around to see the pig on her side. Cruyff went in with a sticking knife, setting off furious thrashing of limbs as the muscles went into spasm and the pig's body slid about in the grit and the blood of the yard.

When eviscerating the innards or cutting away the skin from the fat, Cruyff would hold out his bloody hands to be rinsed. I poured cold water over his knuckles as he grinned at me like Popeye the sailor. Sometimes we gave him already-lit cigarettes which he held in his mouth like a rock guitarist, never touching them with his fingers and once they were spent, he spat out the hot butts sideways onto the flags.

As we finished the pig, there were noises outside and when I told him it was just Petar, he rolled his eyes. We could hear the old man muttering one of his mantras,

'Put that down. Put that down. Don't let him have it. What have I always said? Hold it properly like this. Hold it right.'

It was like an old memory coming to the surface, something that had been said to him as a kid.

'What is the point of that man? He has no work and no woman. What kind of life is that?' Cruyff said, 'He may as well be dead.' And then he crossed himself at the thought of what he had just said.

Once he had split the backbone, the meat came into the house quickly. First the two shoulders, then the ribs, fillet and tenderloin, and finally the two back legs, the precious hams. Cruyff must have felt bad for what he had said against Petar so he suggested that I cook a piece of meat and wrap it and give it to the man hot when he passed by the house that evening. As a surprise treat, *iznenada*.

We had a short coffee at the outside table in the yard and Cruyff talked about his father, the man who kicked him out of the house at sixteen. That was something the two of us had in common. He called his father *muzha* 'The Man' and as he finished rolling the cigarette, he added that he had never seen 'The Man' again. I was not sure whether to believe him. He did not ask me anything about my life, except for questions that needed no answer such as, 'Chris, why do you smoke like a girl?'

What I really wanted to know was whether he felt like a farmer or a nomad but it did not seem right to ask that kind of question. Anyway, my Bulgarian was not good enough to explain the nuance I had in mind. Did I even know the difference? After all, I still think of myself as both farmer and nomad at the same time.

Cruyff did not grow anything in his garden and that was very unusual in a village like ours where every household had a vegetable plot, ploughed in the Autumn and harrowed to a fine tilth in the Spring. But not our Cruyff. He had hunting dogs in there and 40 sheep in the barns. Maybe, he was more of a pastoralist. Anyone who saw him in the forest with a gun, or on the pastures, bare-chested on horseback, surrounded by sheep and dogs, could see that he valued his freedom. They all admired his strength, recognizing the power of the nomad and giving him respect because deep down he reminded them of Asparukh's warriors, the men who had crossed the Danube with their herds and horses in the seventh century.

Cruyff could be reckless and he didn't care about gossip. He had been married once but his wife left him during a brief spell in prison in the 1980s. One day he said to me that he was banged up for having an unlicenced gun and the next for letting his sheep onto the *TKZS* fields so I never knew the real reason. He had two daughters and a grandson but he did not speak to them anymore. He always said that he was free but what kind of freedom was it? There was no point asking him if he was happy or whether he could change the manner of his life because he was no dreamer, just a born survivor. Was that the kind of freedom I wanted for myself?

There is an absolute joy in taking life as it is given and in Podgoritsa that meant living by the seasons. At summer solstice, 21 June, there was a perfect symmetry to the day. The goats spent twelve hours on the pasture and twelve hours at home and they came back in a cloud of dust. Time stood still, as the year settled and adjusted itself around the axis. For Violeta and Simona their thoughts turned automatically to winter. They knew they had to be ready so the work of preparation continued throughout the year.

In June, there was such abundance that you could provide for yourself with little work. Delighted by the harvest, Claire and I wandered along the garden rows and ate the peas and broad beans fresh from the pods. We cut branches of wild green plums and gave them to the goat kids. There were so many courgettes that we left some to grow fat to become marrows but even the pigs were fussy about eating those. At the same time, Simona and Violeta would be preserving and bottling every last vegetable, putting the numberless jars aside for the cold months. They wasted nothing as they tried their best to control time itself. We just let it pass by.

On Midsummer morning, as I arrived at the corner before anyone else, I could feel the weight in the air as the heat built for the day. It was early. Denny walked over with flowers in her mouth and presented to me, the top of her head so I could scratch between the horns. She stretched her head up as the pink petals fell down out of her mouth onto the road. In the summer there was so much variety in the goats' diet. They ate grasses and herbs and fruit and leaves, but in winter it was only *lutserna*, Alfalfa which I gave to them dry, three times a day in the cold stamping stall. Summer was when the sweaty work took place, the cutting and gathering and then the storing of the heaps and bundles of dried *lutserna* for January, February and March. As goat farmers, that was one bit of preparation we were never spared. In the first year I bought a long-handled scythe and did my best to cut the field by hand. Baba Dora watched from the fence and afterwards gave me a small coke. She told me that she used to do that kind of thing in the work brigades. It was exhausting. At the end of the day, she let me know that her son had a machine specially for this job and he came to the village every weekend. I did not need to be told twice.

Dancho took ten minutes to cut the field of *lutserna*, bouncing on his mower up and down over the bumps as the gears jammed or the vicious blades stuck on the wet stalks. I needed two hot days for the piles to dry in the field, turning them twice with a hay fork. Then I would rake it all into piles and carry them into the yard and up into the drying loft. We also needed a few bales of straw but that came from the *Corporatsia* wheat fields. At harvest, a good three weeks before England, the combines worked till late. The road was full of dust and you could feel the ground shake as the massive grain trucks thundered past the house. Once the straw had been baled, the word went out and there were vans and pick-ups outside the gates of the *Corporatsia*. I called Cruyff and the next day, we drove up there in his Lada Niva pulling the cute painted *karutsa*, the wooden horse cart behind as if it were a trailer.

We waited in line and as he talked, I could not help but stare at the pattern of his face, all the scars and cracks, normally bleached out by the sun, were here exposed like a contour map in the shade of the walnut tree. Cruyff's nose was almost a place in itself, black hairs, pock marks and bumps, like his very own patch of rough landscape, neglected like the corner of a field. He told me that, when he was a child, he had been sent away from Krepcha to Golyamo Gradishte. He stole his grandfather's gun and went off into the forest. His baba did not know what to do so she sent a telegram telling his father to come and deal with the boy. They were worried that if he shot someone, the police may have to be called and there would be trouble then, as they had no licence for the gun. I could tell that he was proud of being the subject of a telegram at such a young age.

Once the straw bales were on the cart, we waited by the weighbridge where Vanya was standing to count them out. She had black hair and a pointed nose and her legs were stick thin in drain pipe jeans. Like a gothic bird, she nested in the old collective farm, guarding its interests and keeping the ledgers, scratching away painfully with ink, impressing the numbers indelibly in the columns, then sucking the nib of the pen.

Vanya winced every time Cruyff opened his mouth in case he said something to embarrass her. There was nothing to disapprove in his hunting skills but there were rumours about the way he treated his family and how he had failed to respect his father. This was a conservative village after all. The gossip rebounded from mouth to mouth like metal *topki* in a pin ball machine. Then there was the way he got involved in the Turkish festivals. That is what people like Vanya could not understand even though it seemed obvious, because everybody needs to belong. If you don't find a place in your own group then you have to try to get accepted by another. It is very hard work to be an island.

He turned to me with a grin as he came out of the office. They had been in there together for ten minutes.

'Can you tell she still loves me?' he said.

'Are you still seeing her?' I said, knowing that she had a husband.

'When I came out of prison, we were together and she wanted to get married but I could not face another wedding. She found her cousin, Slavi. He was from the class below

96

and now he is a kids football coach. That sweet guy.'

'And you are free.'

'Of course. I am free. *Svoboden sum razbira se.*'

I wondered then, whether he had ever felt hemmed in by the travel restrictions under Communism. He was a nomad, but not the kind who wandered very far. He had always found freedom inside the pastures and forests and he probably never felt imprisoned because he could always escape to the wild spaces. Vanya and Slavi were definitely settlers by contrast. They grew vegetables. Their chosen animals were chickens and domestic pigs.

A day out with Cruyff was an adventure. One of his hunting pals had called to say there was a horse running wild near the monastery caves and nobody could catch it so Cruyff went off to help. He took me with him. He knew the village boundaries, the invisible lines between the trees and he was one of the few people allowed to chase the animals across them. From the mineral spring where we left the car we walked through tall dry nettles and stumbled like explorers over turrets of dressed stone. The 'Castle of Ghosts' was a Byzantine fortress, built by Emperor Justinian in the sixth century. It was the final attempt to defend the Danube frontier of the Byzantine Empire. Cruyff saw fresh horse dung at the base of the ruined wall. He lit a cigarette and told me that there were two names for the castle, both of them in Turkish, *Buyuk Kale* and *Djinn Kale*. Then we heard the call to prayer stray over from Krepcha mosque and it did not feel like we were in modern Bulgaria at all but a province of Constantinople, caught somewhere in time between the spheres of Istanbul and Salonika.

'The museum in Popovo is scared of people coming with metal detectors. They try to claim that there are two fortresses here but you never know if what they are saying is true. It might just be to fool us. Just like the old days,' he said.

An eagle was circling on the thermal currents and down in the valley bottom, the river looked like two winding ribbons. Cruyff said that he had camped out in the caves that peppered the stone cliffs. On 1 May his classmates used to head out to the woods to spend the night, even the schoolteachers' kids and the Muslim kids.

'We had to climb up the rock face hand over hand. On the last time, I scratched my name in the stone,' he said and pointed to the biggest cave which had been a medieval rock church. These days there were wooden steps for the tourists. We climbed them.

Inside the church a priest in black robes was lighting candles against the shadows. Another man, Kiril, beckoned us inside and said that the museum had paid for a new *ikonostas*, the wooden screen, with the images of saints in bright colours. Kiril, who worked at the museum, asked me a question,

'Where are you from?'

I told him that I lived in Podgoritsa. He fingered the silver cross that hung around his neck on a chain and said,

'It's a very clean Bulgarian village.'

There are two tenth century inscriptions that give this rock monastery its fame. One of them is the oldest surviving piece of Cyrillic writing anywhere in the world. Another inscription reads in translation,

"Whosoever turns this church into a granary will answer to God."

'The people from Krepcha village are not Christians like you and I and they do not always respect our heritage,' said the man from the museum,

'They used to throw rubbish in here and light fires. It was like the inscription coming true. For 500 years we were under Turkish oppression and our holy places were turned into granaries,' he said, giving us the usual line, taught in every Bulgarian school that the Ottoman Empire had been nothing but slavery.

The priest had finished his prayers and was going round extinguishing the candles so we left the place. As we walked steadily down, I thought of teenage Cruyff, climbing up the rock face, his backpack stuffed with *rakia* and cigarettes.

At the bottom of the steps, we said goodbye to the man from the museum and Cruyff rolled his eyes to heaven,

'He can blame the Muslims of Krepcha if he wants but it was the communists who ran the municipality for 50 years. They closed the churches. Why does he not blame them for neglecting our Christian heritage?'

Then he spat on the street to damn the hypocrites and I recognized something of myself in him. I had plenty of chances over an espresso in the garage, to tell him about myself. My uniquely English backstory.

At the age of eight I went off to boarding school. Initially, a keen student I turned slowly from class comedian to clueless rebel and at 15 was expelled for writing a book about one of the teachers. My father, who was Chairman of the Governors of the school told me the news. I remember feeling slightly excited by the drama of it all because suddenly I was out in the world, free to make my own decisions. Pretty soon, I realized I was not free like a bird of prey but un-anchored, on my own like a boat adrift on an unfamiliar sea, 15 years old with absolutely no life plan.

It was 1982 when I discovered punk. In black fishnet gloves, I dyed my hair red and made my own ear rings out of chicken bones. This change in direction was not at all to my parents liking especially when I signed on the dole, left home and rode around Hull on a moped with a broomstick fixed along the top of the exhaust pipe. I found a cheap place to live in a bedsit on Louis Street in the same house where the Hull folk singers, The Watersons had lived in the early 1960s. I did not know that until much later when I saw the bay window of my old bedroom on a grainy documentary. It tied things up because the TV show was made for the BBC in 1965 and that was also the year, I was born in Beverley Westwood maternity hospital, in a building which is now luxury flats.

Back in Bulgaria, each late summer day stretched on forever. We had enough straw and *lutserna* to last the winter but the sun still burned the tiles above the lofts. At this time of year even the nights were hot. I walked up the field road to the ridge. The flies buzzed stubbornly and bothered my bare shoulders and the sunflower heads drooped down to face the ground. The bright yellow flowers had withered as if some toxic rain had leached the field of all its colour. The maize plants were paper dry and the yellow cobs hidden inside the tight coil of leaves. Vanya's bosses in the *Corporatsia* were waiting until every last drop of life had been sucked from the earth, the oil and sweetness distilled in the seeds. Perhaps it was no place to be walking. The harvest team could appear at any minute; the trucks, the combines and the little jeeps with their flashing lights.

At the top of the hill there was a pumping house which before 2005, used to feed the village gardens with water. The irrigation canals criss-crossed the fields all the way from the Cherni Lom to the village. The pipes were dried up now and if you turned on the big tap nothing came out but old air. There used to be a life-giving heart which had, in former times kept the windows glazed, the rooves tiled, the garden walls neatly plastered but, like the sunflowers, the village was slowly dying. Its heart was shrinking and the settlement was thirsty and parched. For the village itself, on its long seasons and cycles it was the end of summer but there was to be no harvest, only lurking violence and broken cars which sat low to the ground and scraped the edges of the pot holes.

I never listened to the Archers when I was in the UK, it was far too middle England but here, a million miles from Ambridge, some part of me needed those familiar voices like an antidote. In Bulgaria, everyone had gone to the west to pick fruit and only the survivors were left, people like Cruyff who lived on nothing but freedom, cigarettes and cheap salami. A plastic chair outside the shop was enough to sit on. Beer bottles were balanced on the bare street.

I waited till the Autumn for my visits back to the UK, so I would never miss out on the thrill and luxury of the deafening heat in August and the light that lasted well into September. Back in Sheffield, everything is shiny. Even in the post-industrial north, the disused buildings do not stay empty long. New student developments have a Tesco Express on every corner. Cranes hang over the waste grounds. There are Chinese students, Indian takeaways, Turkish barbers, folk sessions, quiz nights, salsa classes and stag dos. Dub reggae pulses out from the pubs.

But it is like someone else walking in the park with the grandkids, someone else doing the travelling here not me. My real body, the one with the person inside, is home in the yard standing on the flag stones, grounded. Cutting up the meat, chatting to Cruyff, smoking like a girl and bagging up the pork for the freezer.

10

Punk's Not Dead

According to my parents' generation, boarding school was supposed to prepare us for an independent life. For mum and dad, going away to school was part of their class identity but that kind of thinking was archaic even before I was born. My first day at that school was 20th September 1974. I was eight years old.

I soon got used to the Sunday walks, daily shoe inspections, name tags on clothes, lights out at 8.30 pm and two boys in a bath. I did not complain about the institution at all until I began to notice that school values were very different from the world beyond the gates. Every day we sang hymns praising ancient patriarchy and austere Christian morals. We sat in the school assembly hall with the flags of the army on one side and the pennants of God on the other and little distinction was ever made between the two. I worked really hard for exams until I was about 12. At some point after that, I chose instead to sit at the back of the class and gaze out of the window, thinking of nothing at all.

Eventually I wrote a pamphlet that sealed my fate. *Teach Yourself Teaching* was an attack on my Physics teacher. Come and get me! Look what I did now! See how little I care! I made 20 copies and sold them for 15p in the school bookshop. The headmaster decided that I should be expelled. I was on my own. Is this the part of the story where the wayward kid finds redemption in football or falling in love? It was 1982 and I found Punk. Perfect. I was saved by nothing.

During the early 1980s, if you wanted to listen to music on daytime radio you could choose between the dad rock of Queen or the plastic pop of Duran Duran. There was no space for any alternative. Music was important to us so we had to make a choice to set ourselves apart. I understand now that we could be accused of exceptionalism, those of us whose whole identity was concerned with being different, who deliberately wore nothing but black and spent our dole money on tickets to see Killing Joke. There was no room in the spotlight so we were forced underground. I had been cloistered since I was eight and I had no intention of staying invisible. At first, I went for the gothic look with black cape and red Mohican but by 1986 things had moved on. As I watched the news footage of the police chasing the travellers at the Beanfield I really wanted to be living in a bus too. A few years later my wish came true and I was hanging out with those same people in a forgotten corner of Carmarthenshire, South Wales.

Rural west Wales was the perfect place for outcasts and anarchists because the hidden farms had plenty of space to park the horse trucks and coaches that doubled as people's homes. The travellers were not interested in going back to the land or making their own yoghurt. The people who escaped to Wales in the 1990s from squats in Brighton or Birmingham were not farmers at all but nomads and hedonists, bored of the city, screaming at the sun and standing in the way of control. The currency in which they dealt, was diesel, ecstasy tablets and dole cheques.

These were some of the most conservative corners of Wales. When Nat and I moved in to the village by the sea with our three young kids, we were like aliens parachuted in from the future. But we were normal compared to some of the folk who lived in the heart of the forest. There was one guy who I used to call Genghis Khan because of his black fur hat. He had piercings in his cheeks that looked like silver tusks and a steel bar that went horizontally through the gristle of his nose. At free parties he would stand on the edge of the fire and when people spoke to him, he just seemed to stare ahead. His eyes were dark hollows and one time, when I saw him grin and show his teeth, it was like a row of roughcut diamonds. At the same time his eyes lit up. 'What twisted thing has made him laugh,' I thought to myself.

The parties went on throughout the year, in forests, beaches and farmhouses and slowly I began to feel, that I belonged at the raves more than I did in the college, where I worked as a lecturer. At one party, as the sun came up, we shared a bottle of wine and Genghis Khan told me that his name was actually Marshall. He had been brought up in Gibraltar and, as a teenager, had jumped the train to London to see Crass and the Poison Girls. After that he ended up in a squat in Finsbury Park and never went back. 'These are my family now,' he said.

Punk had saved so many people but where had it come from? There is more than one origin myth even for this. In London, they say that it began in 1976 when the Sex Pistols swore live on the Bill Grundy show but I prefer a different telling. I have always loved the garage bands from the 1960s and I know the early punks were listening to this rough edged rock and roll with a sprinkle of psychedelia. Bands like the Thirteenth Floor Elevators from Texas, The Sonics from Seattle, a whole scene of teenage bands in Los Angeles and the avant garde sounds of the Velvet Underground in New York. The raucous angry kids were pushed off the streets by the L.A. police and the punk essence, soothed and sedated by flower power, but it never went away completely. In the late 1960s, the Stooges and the MC5 kept the sound alive and then it all re-appeared in 1974 in New York. For me, the Ramones at CBGBs was another beginning. Anthony le Bourdain said that seeing them play in that club changed his life forever. Listening to my brother's Ramones records as a teenager changed mine. They sounded like the Shangri Las on speed and their first album set the tone for the Sex Pistols, the Clash and the Buzzcocks who followed. It was not just the music or the fashion. For us the appeal of punk was its energy and its truth. There was a DIY life force and that is perhaps the thing that stayed with me because if you reject authority then you have to organise for yourself.

The DIY ethic is what the travellers in Wales owed to the punks, especially to bands like Crass. By putting on free parties on other people's land, we were making our own entertainment with total disregard for licences or door prices or anything like that. Once punk was taken out of the media spotlight it was no longer nihilistic at all but hopeful and joyful and free. There is the same ethos of independent living in the people who have ended up in Bulgaria, attracted as they are to the empty spaces of deeply rural communities filled instinctively with a healthy folk anarchism.

Even though Bulgaria has a mafia state which controls big business and the media, life can be anarchic at the grassroots and in the village, there are few regulations. In the rest of the EU, if you want to make your own spirits you should really get a licence but here in Bulgaria the rules are ignored. Every village is full of people making their own *rakia*. You can buy a copper still in the market. The bottles of spirit are used as currency and sold in the village shops. Everyone turns up at parties with a bottle of something home-made. There is a surplus. The same goes for rearing animals in the backyard and killing them yourself. No regulations yet. If we were going to translate the DIY ethic of punk to food and drink then it was only going to be possible somewhere like Bulgaria.

There was one hard truth that came with embracing the freedom of the village. Eating our own meat meant killing our own animals and this awful skill we had to learn quickly. As a practical sort who had learned detachment at an early age, I thought it would be straightforward and in theory it was, but some time during our second year, when Violeta asked me to slaughter one of her goat kids, I was terrified at the thought.

'There is no one else to ask,' she said, 'I wanted you to do it last month when I asked you the first time. He is quite big now because I left it so long.'

I wanted more than anything to be a good neighbour to her so I agreed. Reluctantly. At that point I had only ever twice been part of a slaughtering and I had never performed that solemn task alone.

The idea of killing the goat for Violeta kept me awake at night. Pokriv was no longer around to help but still, I asked him for support. When the day arrived, I gritted my teeth, grabbed the knife and chopper and stepped into the heat of the street. She met me at the gate. The first thing we did was to hang swivel-hooks from a low beam above the concrete path. This was where the juices would run. I felt sick. It was worse than any job interview.

Violeta held the kid down, sideways to the ground so I could cut quickly through the skin, the wind pipe and the main arteries. I used a very sharp knife. The life drained away in seconds. Then came the blood. Afterwards, the neck lay open and gory and there was I, standing with the blade in hand, heart beating through my chest. I could feel it pumping at the back of my throat. It stopped me speaking but gave my hands a rhythm to work to.

Pokriv had shown me how to pierce the tendons on the back legs and hook them up high so the head hung down just above the ground. Once I had skinned it and cut the thin belly to the spine, the stomach and intestines dropped out under their own weight. The caul fat was like a net around the stomach and the Bulgarians called it *bulka* after the white bridal veil. My neighbours used it to wrap stuffed cabbage leaves in the oven. But there was another chamber, behind a membrane stretched tight like the skin of a drum. This was the realm of blood and oxygen, high up in the chest where the heart and lungs were kept safe inside a prison of ribs.

Violeta barked orders from the edge of the yard,

'Make a hole there. Wash it off. Do the front legs. Pull the skin down. Slit the breast bone.'

I felt like an amateur.

'Put the *loi* in the bucket. Cut off the ribs. Wash the blood from the innards.'

How small was the heart! How soft were the delicate lungs! I tried my best to concentrate.

Once it was done, she swilled away the blood and it was a shock to see so much red, like spilled paint on the concrete. Violeta took the head and cleaned it to make soup. I handed her the kidneys and the slippery liver with great care so she could place them in a clean enamel pot.

She had seen it all before but for me, it was a new kind of drama. I had read John Berger's *Pig Earth* in which he describes being present at a slaughter in the French Alps, but Berger was an observer and no book could have prepared me for such an active involvement. Not only that, but I was the one responsible for the whole show. Taking a life is a big deal.

Rearing animals for meat was our small act of resistance to factory farming but I never got used to the kill. I felt heavy in the days leading up to it, and afterwards, it was like my energy had been drained. What I had done seemed to be something sacred and it was impossible to take each death lightly, especially when I had been there at the beginning.

The goats often gave birth in the middle of the night. On the due date I never slept well, waking up at midnight and again at 2 am when I might pull on my trousers and boots and go out to check. If I found her half an hour into labour, I would gather up the first born and rub it with a towel to warm up the little thing. The mother sprang into action furiously licking each one of the kids, always working relentlessly to keep them alive. I watched, as under the heat lamp, the steam rose from their shivering bodies. When it was really cold, I put them next to the *petchka* inside the house for a few hours. By the time they went back to the stable, they were full of life jostling for position with all the other siblings. After that, my job was simply to feed the mum and allow her instincts to take over.

Simona's son Todor didn't normally drink but he would take a shot of *rakia* before he killed his pigs at Christmas. For courage. The one time I tried it, the booze dissolved away most of the nerves but it replaced them with a kind of brutal confidence, the bravado of the slaughterman. For that reason, I learned to cope with the kills totally sober because nerves were good for perspective. They helped to remind me that I was not a god.

Animal sacrifice has always been a way to communicate with the divine because the killing opens up a channel to a world beyond. At Demir Baba Tekke on the Thracian altar stones, you could run your fingers down the channels that took away the blood from ritual killings. If you went there on the Christian festival of *Ilinden*, St Ilia's Day or *Gergiovden*, St George's Day, local families would be gathered by the tomb of the Islamic teacher. They roasted lambs on spits and took portions of meat all around the people who were camped, especially the foreigners. They gave us big portions in the spirit of pure hospitality.

My own ritual for those special afternoons when all the butchering was done, was a meal of kidneys, fried in butter with diced chilli pepper and scrambled eggs. After the killings, the garden seemed quieter than usual. There were no more kids in the yard and the only reminder was Belcho barking at the execution spot. He barked a lot but there was nothing left to alarm him except the hooks on a low branch and a patch of dried blood alive with flies on the muddy floor.

The little goats were like guests but once we had killed the males, this part of the season was over. As we took milk every day from the nannies, the walnut leaves began to curl and it reminded me that summer was on its way out and we should start thinking about getting ready for the next one. Within weeks the goats would be pregnant again.

Being a rebel had seemed so important in my old life but here the conditions of dissent were different. In the UK, killing your own animals and making your own whiskey were things you could only do outside the regulations. Here it was normal practice. Was that because, in the village, everyone was a rebel at heart, or that nobody was? Was there even space for dissent in a place like this? The only thing I could be sure of, was that the disregard for regulations and the DIY spirit were common place. Faced with Pokriv's condition and the reality of his death, all of that was less critical anyway. It was survival that mattered. Most people here believed that human life was governed by fate. The best way to live was to carry on going until your last day, then simply give up and, like Wally the dog, allow yourself to melt back into the rich earth.

11

The Writing on the Wall

Simona put up a *nekrolog* poster for Pokriv but it never became permanent like those for her father, her husband or uncle. By dying young, these three men defined the sadness at the core of her being. And it was that emotion which formed the backdrop to her quiet changing moods.

Violeta was the first to come to the house when we found Pokriv's body on the bedroom floor. She opened the windows and made herself busy. All we did was go out onto the street and sit on the bench and breathe some fresh air so it must have been Kuna, his aunt, who rushed home and spread the word by phone. The next day, Violeta took her place in the principal chair by the coffin. By then, Kuna had cleared away all the food from the sideboard, the same food which the day before might just have kept him alive.

I knew all the Bulgarian words around death. How could I not? *Grobnitsa* is grave and *grobishte* cemetery whilst *pogrebenie* means internment, burial and funeral. Funerals were not for the dead at all but for the living. The death ritual was social theatre and it occurred in the domestic space. This elaborate performance included conspicuous grieving, display of solemnity and sadness, the sharing of stories and confidence, unconditional hospitality, cautious presence and deliberate absence. The foreigners even got involved. We all played our part. Funerals gave us a chance to show that we were members of this community, to declare publicly that we were respectful and serious people.

In my own upbringing, protestant and English, we were kept away from funerals but for Claire in Catholic Derry, they were an essential part of the culture and she instinctively knew what to do. When Aladin's mum died we went along, mainly on her insistence, to pay respects to the family. The ceremony brought all the Turkish Bulgarians together in one place. We stood in the street as they brought out the coffin to be blessed by the Imam before the men carried it to the cemetery. Aladin himself found two chairs for us and his wife gave us coffee and sweets and they all accepted us into their hearts, especially the older women. We were the only non-muslims there. After that, people like Biastra and Maya would cross the street to say hello. They still do. They have not forgotten.

Funerals were cracks in the fabric of the world as well as portals between life and death. Most of the British immigrants were keen to integrate and some of my compatriots made a point of attending as many funerals as they could. They followed the local customs, carried the correct number of flowers, made themselves known to the grieving wife, even stood forward and offered to carry the box. Violeta played her role too. By taking the place in that upstairs room she was staring into the face of other people's death and making herself indispensable to its business. Simona was the opposite. She did not want to see anyone else's grief because she had enough of her own. She stayed away.

Pokriv's grave was a mound of earth topped with flowers and candles. Tyre marks had set hard in the clay and the man himself peered out from his own *nekrolog* stuck up on a lamp post, as if he had known all along. The shock was still there in his aunt's eyes as she handed out food for us to take home, *za vkushti* and we stood awkwardly, balancing paper plates. They treated us like old friends because we had made the effort to come, even if we did not always know what to do.

Pokriv did not have many friends but everyone knew him, so there was plenty of people at the graveside. His body went straight from the house to the cemetery. We left him in the ground and walked down to the restaurant.

On the wall of the apartment block, someone had written '1919' in big black letters, the date of the Treaty of Neuilly, which had sealed the fate of Bulgaria after the First World War. On the opposite wall there was another date in fresh paint, '1937'.

The long table was full of people from the village but nobody knew who was paying for the unlimited drink. When Svetlo sat down to talk I asked him about the dates on the wall. He took a good sip of *rakia* before beginning to speak. At the same time, Troy appeared on my other side. He was a neighbour from the village but originally from Wales and he used to play Bob Dylan songs in the bar on his guitar. He leaned over and said something that sounded like complaining, in my other ear. At the same time Svetlo said,

'My wife's grandfather was about 20, so they got him making the concrete pillar on top of the *mogila*.'

That was the mound we could see from the village which featured in so many stories.

'And the reason he met the King himself was that he had an accident doing the wooden shuttering and lost one of his fingers.' He looked at his own hand and flexed his fingers into a fist.

Troy picked up the Rizla packet from the white tablecloth,

'You know why Rizlas are called that don't you?'

I tried to block him out so I could hear Svetlo who said,

'Her grandfather always said that his fingers were cut off by "this very knife" which became a family joke even though it wasn't strictly true.'

He wiped away the sweat. Nobody had been sitting at the head of the table because the sun was shining right onto it like a spotlight.

'Well just take a look at the packet. *Riz La* and then a cross. See that?' said Troy. Then he took a big gulp and his mouth changed, and he grinned and bared his teeth and swallowed it down. The man across the table looked over and pulled an admiring face.

'It's French. *Riz* means rice as in rice paper. And *croix* is cross but the important thing is that Lacroix is the name of the man who first marketed the rice paper for cigarettes. So it is actually *Riz La Croix* but they replaced the word *croix* with a cross on the packet and it became Rizla +.'

I filled our three glasses from the jug. Troy to my right and Svetlo to my left. One on each side. I did not know where to turn my face so I just stared ahead, both ears open wide.

'I suppose you can say this about every country but I can only speak for my own and I know we are proud of our army. Vietnam was a long way from America and Iraq too. I think that as a country we Bulgarians believe in peace. When I joined the army I told them I was from Popovo and they all knew the town because of King Boris and the Royal Manouevres. So that is why history still means something to us and why those dates were written together on the wall.'

Svetlo coughed and then quickly sneezed so hard his nose went watery and red,

'1937 was the year of the military manoeuvres and 1919 was the treaty that destroyed us. Those are the dates on the wall.'

Then he added,

'But don't forget that 1919 is also the date for the Chernolomets Popovo football team so it could have something to do with that.'

He smiled brightly and paused, giving us a chance for all three to clink our glasses and say *nazdrave* as if it were a party.

'You're an archaeologist,' Svetlo said, not even as a question.

'Yes I used to be.' I said and he laughed.

'You can't "used to be". Either you are or you're not. There is no "used to be" in things as serious as that.'

In October 1937 the entire Bulgarian ruling elite had descended on Popovo in a fanfare of flowers and newsreel cameras. All the government ministers, the royal family, the patriarchy of the church and most of the army came over from Sofia. It was a show of patriotic strength and an attempt to recover from the unforgiving cruelty of the Treaty of Neuilly whose demands in 1919 had been so harsh on the country. Popovo town was the centre for the parades and banquets but it was an expanse of common land called Shabantsa outside Podgoritsa that they chose as the field for the headquarters and the military co-ordinations.

In 2017, Popovo Museum wanted to mark the 80 year anniversary so they organized an exhibition of photographs from the archives and commissioned a new statue of the King to be unveiled in the town centre. It was to be, and still remains, the only bust of King Boris in the whole country.

At the exhibition, there was something hopeless about the images from 1937. Maybe it was the cavalry with the coloured banners or the officers in ridiculous jodhpurs as if nothing much had changed since 1878. I tried to recognize the places where the troops were marching, the parade of vehicles trundling through Popovo, the heavy trucks beneath a floral arch, and the King himself taking flowers from schoolchildren. Everyone was in uniform like in a fascist country. In the exhibition space nobody wanted to speak too loud as if the event had become sacred or because the manoeuvres had been sleeping for so long that they should not be disturbed. The event was not something the communists had ever wanted to remember. The pictures had been sealed in a box in the museum archives with all the rest of the 'bourgeois' material. And still it seemed that people did not really know how to handle these memories. Even now.

As I stood in front of the photographs, a few weeks after the funeral, a man tapped me on the shoulder and said hello with a handshake. It was Svetlo. He pointed to the photograph and said in my ear,

'*mogilata*. Podgoritsa.'

He read out the caption for the image in a whisper. The picture showed a scaffold on top of the burial mound, the shuttering for the concrete signal tower. This was the highest point for miles and, from here, the observers could keep track of the two sections of the army, one advancing from Byala the other from Razgrad.

The grandfather of Svetlo's wife had helped to build the tower on top of the mound which was also, of course, the setting for the execution of Princess Antola, the legend so beloved by Simona and the place where she had met her Stefan. Svetlo led me round the gallery and pointed out places I knew where the goats grazed. There was a picture of the King at the parade ground and next to him his brother Prince Kiril who after Boris died in 1943, was part of the wartime regency government. Two years later, on 1 February 1945 he was tried by the Peoples Court and executed along with thousands of others.

In 1937, the land for the parades and inspections was an open pasture, a great *polyana* where the village herds used to wander. There was nothing to mark the field these days because the manoeuvres had been deliberately left out of the story of the village. Old apple trees now cover the site. When I asked Rumi about it one morning over herbal tea she said it was too long ago to remember. As far as she was concerned there was nothing to share. She was quiet for a bit and then filled the gap with a story about the May Day parades of her youth, everyone marching in classes and professional groups with flags and sashes. Without a trace of irony. This was what she wanted to remember not some show of semi-feudal glamour from the time of fascism, or a visit to the village by a long dead king, the friend of Hitler.

Svetlo had promised to show me all the places on the photographs and one day in October he turned up at the house in a battered VW polo so we could walk across the bridge by the poplars, past Krainik's polytunnels and out of the village. From the grove of cherry trees, we looked over fallow sunflower fields and Svetlo told me that this was where his grandmother and her sisters used to do the *Peperuda*, the Butterfly. Every year, the women made a baby out of mud and rolled it around under the bridge, singing songs to encourage the rains to come back. As soon as we went away from the village, memories like these came to the surface because there was no litter of ruins to keep them down.

An hour later we had reached the plateau and the *mogila* itself.

'Do you know what the king ate at the banquet in the city garden in Popovo? A single egg. That's all he had. And it was a Podgoritsa egg,' Svetlo said, 'These are the words of the King, "it is enough for me to have this and nothing else because I do not want to spoil its taste. I will savour this egg forever." That is what my father told me.'

Then he pulled out a package from the inside pocket of his leather coat and unwrapped it carefully. First, he laid the layers of soft cloth on the ground and flattened them out. Then he showed me the photograph with its ornate shiny frame. He unfastened it at the back and there was another one inside. One of the pictures was King Boris in his military uniform and ceremonial sword and the other was Boris' baby son Simeon born in the same year, 1937.

'My father always said that he believed in the workers, so he was pretty much a communist at heart. Why he kept this I don't know. I guess he was a proud Bulgarian.'

Dobri the Mayor was sitting behind a table getting ready to address the meeting. The room quickly filled up and by the time he started speaking there were people standing in the doorway. Stefan Bees told me that years ago, he used to dance in this room and the line of dancers would wind out onto the beautiful terrace at the back of the restaurant. At the meeting, the Turkish women all sat together including Kaimet who was not wearing her head scarf and I think it was the first time I had ever seen her dark hair, streaked stylishly with grey. Dobri went over all the things that his workers had done. They had cleaned up the cemetery, cut down all the plums and acacias and sprayed the whole place with Roundup. They had also cleared the garden by the old nursery and equipped a room with table tennis for the kids.

They had cut the hay from the football pitch and sold it off for bales to raise money for the bridge repairs. Kaimet's grandson had done this work for free. When Dobri said that he wanted to clean up the old mosque building it was as though he had spoken something secret, but the ripples of whispering sounded like approval too, after all this time.

At the end of his prepared speech, he looked up from his script and asked if anyone had any questions, reminding them that they were free to say whatever they wanted as we were living in democratic times. One of the older women at the back stood up and said something about the dogs in the street, asking whether she was allowed to put down poison or shoot them. Dobri calmed down the laughter and told her that she must not use a gun in the village and poison was a bad idea because of the cats and other animals that might eat it.

'How should I get rid of them?' She said.

'They probably belong to some of your neighbours,' Dobri said.

'She knows they do, that is why she is asking,' said another woman.

Then the audience talked itself to a clamour and Dobri had to quieten them down before looking around for more questions.

'Is anybody going to the unveiling of the King's statue today in Popovo? I would like a lift,' said a man at the back.

Hilarious laughter erupted from the audience and everyone left the room beaming with delight, even Dobri. I asked whether he was going to see the unveiling himself, and his grin broadened further and he slapped me on the back as if to say there are many things you do not understand Chris but I will forgive you for being so naïve.

I went along to the ceremony anyway to see for myself because it made me feel like a journalist. The site for the new statue was the same spot where Boris had met the Governor of Shumen in October 1937, exactly 80 years before. I did not want to get mixed up in the fervent group of believers gathered between the two rival kebab shops so I went into the trees where the old men played chess on summer afternoons. There were other observers there, away from the bust and plinth which was shrouded in a blue cloth, waiting to be unveiled. I sat next to a man who shifted up on his seat, holding his stick in front of his knees. He winked and offered me a chocolate because it was his birthday. We said nothing for a few minutes, just watched the people waiting for the dignitaries to arrive with the priests, the boy soldiers and the Patriarch of the church.

I never stand up during national anthems. Even my own. John Berger, the English writer who lived for many years in France, considered himself to be a 'patriot of elsewhere' which I can understand although I would prefer to be a 'patriot of nowhere', that is no patriot at all. The man on the bench next to me blamed his poor knees so the two of us stayed put while everyone else got up, even the mums with the buggies. After that he gave me another chocolate and leaned over to talk while everyone watched the soldiers marching. Down in the market, life went on as normal. The families selling grapes and pumpkins were not perturbed. It was Friday after all.

The time had come for him to show me something. He clasped his hand on the marble plinth next to us and told me to look up. It was another statue. This town had so many. The name on this one was Mara Taseva with her dates, 1900 to 1942. She died the year before Boris. Mara Taseva had been a communist organizer in the 1930s, a rebel activist for her times and was sentenced to death for supporting the Partisans. Unlike other women in her position she did not receive a pardon and this made her the first woman in Bulgaria ever to be killed in this way. After 1990 Popovo Municipality had decided to keep the statue because of the strength of feeling that supported her memory in this town. You could call it nostalgia but it was more clear cut than that, something simply humane. Nobody liked the state sanctioned killing of a local woman. The Popovo mayor knew his own people. After all he had been re-elected five times since 1990 and that made him the longest serving mayor in the whole of Bulgaria.

In the village, much of the past was never commemorated. The events just hung around the street corners and trees. Maybe the memories moved with the seasons or died when the people died. Every empty building became its own memorial but only if you knew the secrets. The old shops and bars had never been restored and you can see what purpose they served by looking inside at the objects on the floor. The Mosque had withdrawn into itself and only a few heads knew the names for the village pastures, the *polyani*, mostly overgrown with creepers and shrubs.

When they look up at the *mogila* in the distance people here still instinctively reach for the legend of Antola and in doing so they fail to recall its actual history, its ancient origins and the role it played in the events of 1937 and the King's visit. The social memory of the Royal Manoeuvres has never been allowed to grow and, suppressed for three generations it is hard to ever bring it back. History is rarely about the truth of what actually took place. It is just the story we choose to tell, the one that suits us.

12

1923

By late afternoon, the meal felt drunken and chaotic like the end of a festival and that was odd for a village funeral. Pokriv would have hated it. Troy and Svetlo were fighting over the tobacco pouch, snatching at each other across the table. When the packet burst open, tobacco flew all over the empty plates of food and into the small shot glasses. A group of Pokriv's neighbours got up to leave and we went outside to help them jump start the van. I looked at the man next to me as the two of us rubbed the dust off our hands. He had a large wiry beard and introduced himself to me as Robin. I told him that was my middle name. Then, as we walked back inside, he took out his tobacco tin and handed it to Troy,

'Try that mate,' he said, 'Bulgarian home grown, from the Rhodopi Mountains. And I do not mean weed. This is actual tobacco.'

'So what brings you here?' I asked, thinking he might just be a passer by.

'Ach! he was my father,' he said and began to roll a cigarette, 'we lost touch years ago.'

I could hardly believe it. The man before me was Pokriv's estranged son. They had not seen each other in ten years.

'I heard from my cousin, over there. We live in Berlin,' And then he pointed to an older woman who was ignoring everyone, reading a book at one of the outside tables. She wore a patchwork flat cap and huge spectacles that made her look like an owl.

'What about yourself? How did you know him? You're English right? From Podgoritsa?'

'We have goats and he likes to talk to foreigners,' I said, unsure why I was using the present tense.

As we walked back in, Troy and Svetlo were still arguing. They cleared the plates and glasses from the table so they could arm wrestle. Staring full in the eyes, they gripped each other's hands until the knuckles glowed white through the skin. We took up a few seats inside the restaurant, in a quiet corner where you could stay all night and I was surprised to check my phone and see that it was only 6 pm at this point. Funerals are usually more sedate than this. We ordered more free drinks, Troy and Svetlo rolled cigarettes for each other, the cousin continued to read her book while Robin and I talked about politics and history and the films that he was making for Youtube.

'The dates on the wall mean nothing at all.' He said, but I was not sure exactly what he was talking about. 'The dates on the wall. I heard you talking with that village guy. 1937. You would never see it in Sofia you know. It's a Popovo date. Somebody must still support the King. And he's right about 1919. It's probably for the football team. But you never know. The Treaty of Neuilly weighs heavy. This country has a long memory. They promised Bulgarian access to the Aegean Sea but it was never granted. Listen to me going on like some old man. I don't care about that shit.'

The dates on the wall. They are a way of telling history. In code. As graffiti.

'Take 1923.' Robin said, 'Sometimes you see it up there on the walls of small Bulgarian towns. It's part of national memory. The communists had tried to overthrow the right wing government in September but the coup failed. So, once they came to power 20 years later, the memory of 1923 was a kind of martyrdom and a reason for vengeance. That's why people paint it up there. But so much else was going on then. Give me a light man.'

'Between the wars? In 1923? Modernism?'

'You know Ernest Hemingway was in Paris, after the First World War, writing about Bulgaria? He was correspondent for the Toronto Daily Star. But the biggest news of all is another uprising in that same year, the one that actually did change the government but nobody goes on about that. The right wing coup against the Agrarian Prime Minister, Stamboliiski. He was like our very own Lloyd George. And that coup had been successful. Hang on. That's my phone. Go and find out. See for yourself. Go to Slavovitsa. Find Aleksander Stamboliiski. The flashing one over there. I can hear it. I left it on the table.'

My own politics started at school. In the face of hypocrisy. Every Sunday we went to church. All of us uniformed boys on the stone-paved streets of Pocklington, walking by classes and houses in our shiny black shoes. Inside the church, nothing much had changed since the 1920s. The vicar wore a white cassock. Sometimes the cadet officers marched down the aisle with flags. It always seemed strange to me that the army should parade inside the church.

Most of the etiquette was unwritten. When it was time to pray we did not put our hands together like angels, all of us boys leant forward in our seats and bent down, heads close to the ground like slaves. I was about 12 on one special Sunday when the hymn finished and the vicar spoke. Hundreds of boys bent forward with a massive shuffling and hushing. Some looked at their shoes, most had their eyes clenched tightly shut but I just sat there, upright in my chair. By then I knew that I should be allowed to pray in any way I wanted and even to have no faith could not be disallowed. It was not like misbehaving or breaking a rule, it was a matter of conscience. The rows and rows of bent bodies and grey jackets with their splits at the back were all around me like a small sea. I stayed where I was throughout the long prayers, looking around like a tourist in a new city, half expecting a tap on the shoulder and a whispered urgent order but nothing came. After that I never knelt forward again. I sat through all the prayer sessions in all the church services I ever attended. It was a tiny cry for freedom. Perhaps the first. I told Robin the story before he rushed away,

'A real English public school boy! I have to go now. Family business. I have not seen my baba for over ten years. She is gonna kill me. My aunty's calling again.' With that he waved to us all, gathered up his tobacco tin, grabbed his cousin by the hand and walked out.

Aleksander Stamboliiski's reputation has suffered because history has always been written by his opponents. Nobody wanted to mention the things that defined him: his opposition to Nationalism and war; the promise of land redistribution; rights for refugees and minorities; his violent death. Faced with selective memory and a politician I might just have time for, I took Robin's advice and made arrangements to go to his heartland and find out for myself.

It was early on Saturday morning when I drove into the square in the centre of Slavovitsa. The bar was closed but four men were sitting around a table with a 2L coke bottle filled with honey-coloured *rakia*. I asked them the way to Stamboliiski's house and they pointed up the hill where a sign read, *Rodna Kushta na Aleksander Stamboliiski*, the birth-place home of Aleksander Stamboliiski. The door was locked so I went off to find someone with a key. No joy. Back around the table the men looked at me kindly with tired, curious eyes. Phonecalls were made and sunflower seeds spat onto the street. It was already very hot. Eventually, a woman walked up and handed me a mobile phone. The voice on the line told me that he was the caretaker of the museum.

'But I was there a minute ago,' I said, 'The gate is locked.'

I remembered the words I had read on the sign and wiped the sweat from under my cap.

'Not that one. That is his family home. The villa is where I am. His villa. *Villata*.'

I must have looked totally confused because the man next to me finished the *rakia* and picked up his car keys, '*haide momche*, let's go.' And he drove me out of the village.

The villa stood in its own grounds looking down towards Plovdiv and the distant Rodopi mountains. In the haze, the flat plain of the valley was almost like the sea. The house was unusually tall with casement windows and a porch that gave it a gothic flair. There was tragedy in the air. You could see it in the architecture. After spending some time in the small basement museum they took me to another building, an out house. I had to stoop to go inside. I was not prepared for what they showed me.

The two men stood in the far corner of the room which was bare except for a plaque on the wall. They took off their hats and as my eyes grew accustomed to the light, it dawned on me where I must be.

This is what English historian Richard Crampton wrote in his book *A Concise History of Bulgaria,*

'On 9 June 1923 an efficiently organized coup deposed the BANU (Agrarian National Union of Bulgaria) government. Stamboliiski was at the time at his home in Slavovitsa. He went into hiding but was discovered on 14 June, tortured, mutilated and finally beheaded; it was said that his head was sent to Sofia in a biscuit tin.'

I was standing in the very same summer kitchen where Stamboliiski, the Bulgarian Prime Minister was killed by Macedonian nationalists. He scrawled the first letters of his family name in cyrillic '*C T*' and the year '1923' on the wall, in his own blood. The fading daubs, no longer red but tawny brown, were still there. None of the books I had read showed photographs of the death marks but they were real enough. The yellow plastic film on the windows had preserved the graffiti from the sunlight for nearly 100 years. His followers had kept his memory alive to never forget that the VMRO cut off one of his hands and fingers and that they severed his head and posted it to King Boris.

At 12 noon the four men were still there round the table. This time I sat down with them and they poured me a *rakia*. Vasil knew what I had just seen and he wanted to tell me something. I could see the fire in his blue eyes but his friends tried to shout him down.

'This gentleman doesn't want to hear your stories,' they said as they filled up his glass with more booze. Vasil stood up in the heat and put on his straw hat and beckoned me to come with him to meet the family. He said that his son could speak English.

Stamboliiski's political impulses have a contemporary edge because they were anti-establishment. There is something defiant and independent about him and Hemingway could see it. He wrote of Stamboliiski,

'He is chunky, red-brown faced, has a black moustache that turns up like a sergeant major's, understands not a word of any language except Bulgarian, once made a speech of fifteen hours duration in that guttural tongue and is the strongest premier in Europe, bar none.'

The Bulgarians were the most influential of all the European Agrarian parties and they were the only ones to ever form a government. Both he and Lloyd George believed in social reform but Stamboliiski's domestic programme was far more radical. It set him against the church, the monarchy and the military. He said that the old parties were, *'parasites on the body of the nation. They have to die: they will die and the sooner the better.'*

He was an enemy of the system who did not try to hide it and that did for him in the end.

By 1948, the Agrarians had been consumed into the communist structure but there was a time when they had their own voice and for a few years after the First World War they ruled the country. Hemingway called Stamboliiski, 'a peasant with a king in his pocket.' After June 1923, only the King was left.

At Vasil's house everyone seemed to be busy. His mother in law was peeling potatoes in the shade and his son was looking for tools to fix the car. Vasil cleared a space on the dining table next to a set of glass shelves holding trinkets from all over the world. He repeated the story of the Macedonians coming into the village and stirring up trouble and taking Stamboliiski up to the villa. His son reluctantly translated some of his father's material into English. Vasil's son was a history student from Kliment Ohridski University in Sofia and yet, uncomfortable with the whole episode, he squirmed in his seat and tried to talk about Berbatov the Bulgarian footballer who, at that time, was playing for Manchester Utd.

I asked him, 'Do you think the King knew the VMRO were going to kill him?'

He smiled thinly. 'VMRO? Maybe yes, maybe no.'

'Is this a difficult subject for you to talk about?'

'No, yes, not really.'

'Have you seen the room where they tortured him?'

He began to motion to me that his father was drunk, his hand pretending to drink, then crazy, his finger tapping his own temples. This is how memories die.

With every hot minute that passed I felt stranded between father and son, between their different readings of the same history. One to remember and one to forget. Stamboliiski was an internationalist. He wanted to stop the Bulgarian claims for territory in Aegean Thrace, Macedonia and Dobrudzha and instead to build a Balkan federation of all the nations. This was radical in 1920 and still today does not sit with the narrative of patriotism nor the blanket of nationalism that covers Bulgarian history. That is why we do not see him take his place at the heart of twentieth century memory but hidden in the corners. The VMRO, the organisation who killed him are still around. In fact during the 2010s they were a Nationalist party in one of the coalition governments led by Boiko Borisov and GERB.

In the Autumn of 1920 Stamboliiski set off on a tour of European countries that would last 100 days. He visited England and met with the Prime Minister, David Lloyd George. Stamboliiski's interpreter on that trip was Nadezhda Stanciova and this is one of the many nice things she had to say about him, in December 1919,

"I really like him very much and I have a lot of confidence in him, if Bulgaria will only let him work in peace."

Stamboliiski inspired loyalty. By the time he was assassinated, Nadezhda Stanciova had been posted to the USA to become Bulgaria's first female diplomat but on hearing of the coup against him, she resigned her official post and moved to Europe. She lived in Scotland where, a few years later as a venerable Balkan dame, she was introduced to a young Steven Runciman, about to go out to Bulgaria to research for his first book.

Stoianova was lucky and privileged enough to be able to stay in Britain. She avoided Bulgaria in the period after the 1923 coup when the new regime cracked down hard on the communists, agrarians and anarchists. That is where we find the modernist poet, Geo Milev. Trying to survive in a hostile environment from which he could not escape.

Geo Milev was a young Bulgarian poet who witnessed the events of 1923 at first hand. In 1924 he published his poem 'September' which became the main literary source of memory for the uprising but it also sealed his fate. The poet was 'disappeared' by the Sofia police in 1925 and then thirty years later, in 1954, his body was discovered in a mass grave. They identified it because of the glass eye he wore, following a head wound on the Macedonian Front during the First World War. In 1925, the police had strangled him with wire. Another victim of what Georgi Gospodinov has called Bulgaria's 'undeclared civil war.'

Apart from his poems the best insight into Geo Milev is a novel by Hristo Karastoyanov called *The Same Night Awaits Us All*. The story is based on the real friendship between Milev and the anarchist activist Georgi Sheytanov, a popular rebel constantly on the run from the authorities. Able to raise money at short notice he supported Milev's literary projects including the magazine *Plamuk*, The Flame. After the two coups of 1923, the net tightened on people like Sheytanov but also on creative thinkers like Milev who dared to stand up to the government. By the end of 1925 the year of the bombing of Sveta Nedelya church they were both dead.

Milev's poem is a passionate account of the radical feelings of resistance to everything that was held sacred by tradition. His poems have recently been translated into

133

English by Tom Phillips. To get a clear sense of that uprising we should take away the veil of adoration that was drawn across it in the 1950s by the BKP propaganda. The poem was not an avowedly communist tract. It was a free thinker's response to rebellion and a modernist masterpiece for the Balkans, in the way it echoes the spirit and style of TS Elliot. The poem would have spoken to Stamboliiski, had he been alive, and also, I think, to that 12-year-old boy in the church, surrounded by the tired institutions of England.

DOWN WITH GOD!
From on high, from the endless
bridges of heaven
we'll haul down
that blessed paradise
with ropes and spars
to the grieving
blood–drenched
Earth.

Everything poets, philosophers wrote
will come true!
– No gods! No masters!
September will be May.
Human life
will be an endless ascent
– higher and higher!
E a r t h   s h a l l   b e   H e a v e n –
it shall!

(Geo Milev, Excerpt from September 1924, translated by Tom Phillips)

When Robin and his cousin went away to see their baba, that left Troy, Svetlo and myself to drink through the night in some apartment and eventually stumble and stagger out onto the street. It was getting light and my head was beginning to hurt. Mornings bring hangovers even without sleep. Troy fell over in the road and was narrowly missed by a minibus carrying workers to the fields. Svetlo tried to hail a taxi which turned out to be a police car. Luckily the officer was his neighbour and within minutes another car arrived to take us home. I fell asleep on the back seat but then woke up to see Troy leaning forwards to try and punch Svetlo in the face. The driver kicked us out next to the raspberry fields where the pickers had just arrived in the minibus and were all sat on the ground eating bread watching us.

We were walking in single file beside the road towards the village when six dogs came running down from the fruit tree farm. The three of us ran off in opposite directions. Somehow I found myself at my own front door so I opened it and fell inside. The cow shepherd must have been watching. I know this because he reminds me every time, I see him. In my head that morning as the sun rose over the park, I saw the bright colours from the front of the guest house. Innocent colours, orange and blue painted there in 1925, the year that the bomb exploded in the roof of the Sveta Nedelya church. I tried to fall asleep on the settee and in my unsettled dreams wondered how Ernest Hemingway could possibly have found his way into this story. The only noise in the street was the cow man shouting but this faded slowly away and the day began. Hangovers fade. Memories too.

13

Dystopia

The next time Lily came to the village, my granddaughter was getting used to the dust, the flies and all the strangeness she had noticed on her first Bulgarian holiday. She seemed to be taking it all in her stride. We carried the storybook into the goat shed like the last time, as if she had never been away. Maybe Grampops' house wasn't so far from her normality after all? Or even so different? Or was it just that I was getting used to it too?

It was Autumn and the wind had blown the last of the walnuts down and Lily and I watched Belcho as he cracked them open letting the shells drop onto the road so he could pull out the nut pieces with his teeth. It was the day of the village festival, the *Sabor* when the exiles returned. In every house they would throw open the doors and set extra places for unexpected guests. When we saw Violeta at the goats that evening, she was all dressed up in her warm clothes for the concert.

According to Margarita (Milk and Honey), the *Dom Na Kultura* had not been full like this for 15 years. The bright stage was packed with people dancing in a line that wound happily down the steps into the auditorium itself. Some of the *Anglichani* rushed down from the balcony to join the *horo*. The *Sabor* always fell on the 7 November, close to All Souls Day and on the nearest Saturday all the Christian families would go up to the cemetery to pour wine over the graves. Simona and Krasimira delivered a packet of *pitka* bread, sweets, boiled eggs and wheatgerm porridge to our door, for the dead. Lily laid it all out on the table and could not believe the treats she had in front of her. Later that week after she had flown home, I printed out a photo with her eyes shining, surrounded by sweets and colours in the candle light.

On the Sunday night there was a party in the bar. They packed us into two rooms, with such a small space between the chairs that the dancing quickly became chaotic. On every table there were bottles of *rakia* and brightly coloured soft drinks, *bez alkohol*, in sweet flavours of fizzy pop. Lily fell asleep and her dad put her down in the backroom next to the kitchen so the women could keep an eye. The choir singers were carrying out plates of food and everyone looked red in the face especially Svetlana herself, in a flowing pink dress. Dave the electrician helped himself from the bottles of *rakia* even mixing the different varieties in the same glass. Dimo leaned over to me and said,

'Your friend is going to make himself ill. He drinks like a priest.'

That night I played violin with the band one more time. We moved around the room mixing with the dancers, and the women came up with serviettes to wipe the sweat from

137

Dimo's face so he could carry on playing the accordion. I joined in with the two songs I could remember, *Stapil Dobri* and *Za Branitsa*. During the breathless break between them, I saw Ivelina. She slipped into the kitchen with her head down and then hurried out into the darkness with two big plates of food covered in foil.

A lot of people in the village would look at Ivelina sideways in the street, without moving their heads, just with their eyes. Especially the older ones. There were all sorts of rumours about her. She lived on the other side of the park and one thing I knew for sure was that her husband had lost his job as a shepherd because the trade embargo with Russia had destroyed that part of the market for Bulgarian lambs. The family were short of money so Ivelina came to help us in the guest house once a week and at 11 am, we always sat down for coffee. She took hers black and strong with lots of sugar. That day she spoke about her kids finding work,

'All I wanna do is go away on my own to an island and stay there,' she said, 'but I can't even leave the country. Hristo won't come with me to Targovishte to get a passport for Esme. The father has to sign. Daniel will probably go to Scotland because there, he can get a job with a contract and Maria has a new boyfriend whose entire family work in England so she is thinking about going there.'

Maria and Daniel were two of her grown up kids. Esme was the youngest and one of the very few Bulgarian children who lived all week in the village. Ivelina was sitting on the other side of the table and I offered her a glass of milk and thought how perfect it was to have fresh milk from the goat. She said later that she was thinking about the news that nobody else had been brave enough to tell us.

It had something to do with the old man in thick glasses who lived near the goat farm. He had roses all along the front fence and at the back, there were tall maize plants standing in rows like sentries. The neat garden was usually empty because he stayed indoors most of the day. The first time I saw him was in late summer as I walked past with Simona at 7.30 am. We saw a slow-moving figure in a trilby hat. The old man straightened up and pressed both hands into the small of his back. For a long time, he stood and looked at us and I stared back, then waved.

'His eyes are bad, so the only way to make him see you is to shout his name and then say who you are.' Said Simona.

Once we were out of earshot, she added, 'or if you see him in the street you have to go right up and take hold of his hand. He can hardly see the road in front of him.'

This half-blind gardener came out to work just before dawn but was always back inside by 9 or 10 am because the bright sunlight damaged his eyes even with shades on. After that I used to see him with the goats in the late evenings. He had a whole group of them. And then again at the party in the bar he was sitting close to us in a black leather coat and dark glasses. That is when I heard them whispering but they all shut up before I could listen in. When the half-blind gardener got up for food, Dave turned the coat inside out to check the lining and to see if it was real leather. Then he reached over for another bottle like an actual piss head.

On the day she told me about it, Ivelina was doing the washing up after breakfast and another visiting family were getting ready to go on a bike ride,

'What date is it today, Chris?' she said.

'The eighth.'

'So, when is the tenth?'

'The day I cannot pronounce,' I said, repeating the word with slightly different stress and she looked at me, turning round with both her hands in the sink.

'*Chetvartuk*, Thursday, no wait it's a Friday,' I said, '*Petak*.'

'But not the twelfth, right? Hristo has an appointment.'

I nipped upstairs to check the solar batteries and when I came back down, she told me the news that I did not forget. Ivelina was surprised that nobody had told us before. It had even been on the national bulletin. And then she gave me another big smile as if she wanted to make it better. Just to see some joy in the life that was left behind.

'Last week a woman was attacked here in the village. I know her family. They are good people. She is in hospital. The bastards who did it are in prison.'

She was a Turkish woman from Ribnovo and the men were Bulgarians from Podgoritsa. I knew the faces and names. Every day these men drank beer outside the shop.

That evening during milking, a scratch on Denny's udder had opened up and when my fingers squeezed, it forced out a line of blood drops along the graze but she did not flinch. I wondered if it was still ok to use the bloody milk but then the red spots blended in and disappeared. From red to pink and back again to white.

'One of those men tried to send Esme a friend request on Facebook,' Ivelina said.

'The school bus driver has refused to stop in the centre now. He does not trust anyone. So, Esme must walk all the way home from the spring which makes it even more dangerous.' The village streets no longer felt safe.

It must have happened on one of those perfect still evenings when we sat under the grapes listening to the silence, watching the sun dip over the hill. Oblivious. Now it felt wrong to enjoy the peace because we had no idea what might actually be taking place behind it, within it, maybe even because of it.

'Kris. Do you really want to stay in a place like this?' Ivelina said, 'I just want to be somewhere safe for my girls.'

But then she smiled again and gathered her bags and told me a story about her English neighbour chasing a dog around the garden in his pajamas and then she went outside into the street to carry on with her life.

I went for a walk to clear my head and gazing across from the ridge, the village looked upside down. The sky was like a sheet of liquid porcelain and the little details of the village were blurred, as if the green leaves were complicit, in the way that they could conceal things. Nothing about this place had actually changed but everything was different.

When I asked my neighbours about the incident, Krasimira and Simona pretended not to understand. They didn't want to talk about it. At first I was confused by their reaction because I knew them to be caring and sensitive people but then Claire reminded me that, like all of us, they must be traumatised. The next day, Simona came round with peppers. It was her way of trying to make it all ok again. I was grateful. I said thank you and made them into a curry.

It was a shock to know that something so violent and abusive had happened right here in the village. I knew that all the people were the same as before, with their smiles and humour intact. The village had not changed and yet it seemed to me so totally different, like a place without hope. Where had all the laughter gone? And the joy and the fun of cracking jokes in the street. All of that had been sucked back into the houses.

The village sounds echoed against a backdrop of deadly quiet. I could hear chainsaws half a mile away. It was something to do with living in a valley. A tractor ploughing gardens. Loud men's voices. Then as the sun went down the dogs would bark in a mad chorus but after the news we listened to the same things differently, waiting for the harsh words or the police sirens or the screams.

It settled like a shadow over us all. The men who sat outside the shop no longer stared so hard at every passer by but instead they looked away or down at the ground. Ray told me that they had thrown Dobri no teeth out of the bar because he had been one of the four accomplices in the car.

'Are you sure?' I said in genuine surprise.

I saw Dobri no teeth a few days later by the bridge and he was walking with a strange movement of his shoulders as if they were too heavy for his body. Then further on down the road I stopped to let the cows go past and saw the leather coat man, the blind gardener, wandering in the street outside his house,

'*Momcheto mi. momcheto mi,*' he said, 'my boy, my boy.'

He looked different. His hair was shorter. He stooped forward in clothes that seemed far too big for him. He had no socks on, just feet straight into black galoshes. I asked about the goats and he narrowed his eyes trying to understand.

We stood there together watching the cows go out and Bogdan signalled from his tractor cab to make sure that we waited and he pointed to his eyes and then to the old man. Once they had gone, I set off but he turned and went back into the house,

'My boy. They have him locked up,' the old man said.

His son. The man who parked his car in front of the house, whose beer bottles were still lined up along the low wall. He had been one of the two guilty men. Both of them were now in Shumen jail.

Whenever there were crimes like burglary or violence, the old people always blamed the 'gypsies', *tsigani*, like Ivelina and her family. This time they could not blame *tsigani* because everyone knew who had done it and it was definitely not *tsigani*. We wanted to live somewhere free, with more space between the regulations but places like that can also be lawless. Most of the young people had gone, leaving behind a skeleton crew of resilient characters, a dwindling band of lonesome pensioners and a bunch of foreigners who just wanted to be left alone.

Before she went home, Ivelina announced that Simona's baby had been born three months early and she was in the hospital in Bristol.

'And Kris', she said, 'it is not like the hospital in Popovo where you have to take in your own sheets and give 8 leva per night. In England the hospitals are warm in winter, too warm in fact, and you don't even have to pay for food. They give you three meals.'

Simona was learning English so she could talk to the nurses.

'I hope she stays there,' Ivelina said.

Ivelina had missed the birth of her grand daughter and there was absolutely no way she could travel to see her. Her other grandkids in Italy were not learning Bulgarian at all and their families did not even want to come back. Especially now. Whenever she dwelt on her misfortune during one of her sad half hours over coffee, she would always finish the cup and pick herself up and smile as if to leave it all boxed up somewhere and then she would tell me some joke about horses. As if there was always hope.

It was all connected. Ivelina could see it and so could I because we shared that outsider's perspective. The broken buildings in the village, the casual poverty, and the incident which had shocked us all, were symptoms of the same thing. A kind of darkening shadow that she ducked away from but could never destroy. A shadow that hung over Bulgaria like unresolved trauma. In her eyes, if only she could get away to the UK it would all be fine. There would be bright skies. Happy people.

I said to her, 'but Ivelina I am just like you, miles away from my grandkids.'

She looked surprised, 'You have chosen this Kris. You can go back to them whenever you want. This is my home and I am stranded. You have a British passport. Your hospitals are free. If you go home, they will give you money.'

Joining the EU had allowed young Bulgarians to work in the rest of Europe and they had left in great numbers because they could see nothing for themselves here. Whatever anyone said about the boom of IT jobs in Sofia, it may as well have been happening on another planet for people like Ivelina. Bulgaria's minimum wage, the freedom of the press, electoral fraud and state corruption under GERB and the other pro-European centrist parties were at the wrong end of the European scale. Since 1990 the population had dropped from nine to seven million and forecasts showed that by 2050 there could be as little as five million people left in the country. Including the *Anglichani*.

The walls of the village were closing in so I went to the mountains to finish writing the final chapters. Elena is a bucolic place in the foothills of the Balkan, the Stara Planina mountain range that runs across the middle of the country from the Black Sea to the Serbian border. The houses here were made from slabs of wood as if built by giants. After two days of walking through its luxurious damp meadows I was suffering from a prickly rash all over my neck and arms. I think it was from nettle stings. The only thing that would distract me was to write all day on the oak-planked balcony where they hung the dry-cured hams. At night I watched the BBC dramatization of the Chernobyl disaster. As I lay there trying to sleep, all I could see were the Soviet firefighters in their hospital beds, faces wrapped in white bandages, eyes staring out in fear.

All horror films have some kind of overarching evil. For the BBC telling of the Chernobyl story, this was not the danger of radiation but the cover up, the silence of the Soviet authorities. Gorbachev often said that Chernobyl brought down the Soviet Union because it confirmed what people suspected, that you cannot go on lying forever. In the end it is lies that kill. Lies about the past and lies about the present. And it was not just clouds of radiation that smothered the former eastern bloc but clouds of poverty and hardship and clouds of selective memory that did nothing but obscure the future.

When the western media looks back at Soviet times, it sees nothing but dystopia and anti-freedom but we should remember that this period and these places had been a lived present for millions who did not all see it like that. In the 1970s they thought a lot about the future and in Bulgaria it was often portrayed in fiction and propaganda as a technological and political utopia. How would Simona and Violeta, and all the people who lived through those years, have seen this present, today in 2022, our present, if they could have flashed forward in time from 1974? Not just the state of the roads but also crumbling hospitals and railways, oligarchic greed at the top of government and an exodus of young people to the west. For the generation brought up under Communism this version of the future, must be the last thing that they ever expected.

Sometimes I want to deny that I am an archaeologist because I know that the past holds us back. It can be too soft and too comforting and can cover your face like a cushion. There is a certain feeling when you wake up later than normal and it is already light, when you are smothered by sleep and confused by the fallout from your dreams and when you are trying to start the day but first you have to get reality straight. That feeling to me is exactly like working out which version of the past is the one you should follow and how much it means to you. Sometimes I want to think like a modernist and start everything again from year zero and to banish all tradition because I know that the past and the history we tell of it means little, because it is so malleable and can be re-framed to suit the conditions of the present. Even here in the village. Especially here.

Three days before Christmas as darkness fell, the *Koledari* came into the house. The five men were huge inside the living room and their boozey voices filled every single corner with sound. They wore thick cloaks and held tall wooden staffs with sprigs of box leaves that sprouted from the handles. They had been wassailing all day, drawing on folk traditions to give health and happiness for the coming year. Trying to make everything ok.

When I used to play in the band it was the old festivals I liked the best. The ones that reached back into the distant centuries, like *Trifon Zarezan* and the *Koledari*. I could see the parallel with the old English festivals like May Day and Imbolc and Halloween. They have a timeless magic that is reassuring and keeps you grounded but it can also be transcendental and mystical.

After the incident all of this just seemed hopeless. Pointless. For a while that was my new take on all of it; the music, the costumes, the ceremonies. On Christmas Eve Claire and I were at the far edge of the village in the big pasture looking at the rough stones of the Muslim cemetery. We spotted the *Koledari* again wandering about and singing in a group. From there we walked along the edge of the *polyana*, dotted with derelict houses and past the old mill and the *rakia* distillery and the sheds by the lake. The gang of costumed men were pretty drunk but they carried on looking for someone to bless, picking over rubble piles to find one more house occupied by the few people who were left. Three of the five men lived in Germany and they had come back for the holiday. They were casting spells to keep the place from dying, reaching back to old certainties, to try and transform the future. But everyone knew this magic was not powerful enough to bring the young people back nor to undo the crimes of the Autumn.

It was not in my power to repair the roads or to find jobs for Ivelina's kids. All I could do was concentrate on the things that happened every day, the small comforts and the routines, over and over again. Slowly healing. When the sun rose every morning it was still beautiful and each evening as it dipped behind the walnut tree there was a different shade of pink or orange or deep red. We could still hear the music and tap our feet in time and we could still hear the birds singing and give each other gifts and do each other friendly favours and pass the time by chatting across the garden fence. And that was exactly how we all did our bit to heal this place.

Even though it was late December the goats were still going out and as the day ended, the temperature dropped with the sun. One evening, the day after Christmas, was unusual as all the different herds came back at the same time and there were five of us waiting, instead of the usual three. Fatme was there for the sheep and Bogdan for the cows. He and I were good at being silent in each other's company and when he smiled with his crooked teeth there was always a twinkle of something in his eyes. His wife Fatme was talking to Violeta about baking cheese and eggs in the oven for the kids. The cows came back first, followed by the goats and then the sheep so the three herds were staggered in sequence down the long road. We walked back behind our animals, aware of the coming snow. The daily grazing of the goats was like a tide, washing us out and then back in again as if we were the waters of the sea. Was it a glimpse of something older, doing this every day, repeating the patterns of past generations or was I part of something new? Maybe the future should be like that, every day refreshing the present, making it new and wiping away the past from this tired land? I wonder if it would be good for us to do a little bit more forgetting.

New Year's Day was just like any other and I was back at the cow farm for milk. Our goats were pregnant so their milk had already dried up. Bogdan's mum Maya, was there in her headscarf and baggy floral printed trousers to pour it out and take the coins. Her tracksuit top had a stripe down the arm like Simona's and she wore a gold watch, small and square at the wrist.

'This is a land of milk and honey', she told me in old fashioned language, 'It always was and will be so forever,' and then she handed me the plastic bottles filled with fresh milk that warmed my hands all the way back down the road.

14

After Hours at the Museum

The Bulgarians called us the *Anglichani*, the English, even though some of us were Irish, Welsh, Scottish, or even Swedish but I'm not sure what we called ourselves. Expat was a dirty word. The village was in a backwater, far away from Sofia, but still it was full of western immigrants. Over the years we had taken over one of the outside tables in the bar and we gathered there on Friday nights to drink the cheapest beer in Europe. Petar used to come up to the table and the *Anglichani* would buy him drinks until he started shouting. Then in the morning, at the goats, he would be sleeping on the ground in his overcoat.

Roy lived next door to Troy on a street called the First of May. If you can call it a street. It was more like a long field where cars could drive if the ground was not too wet. Roy complained about the wrecked vehicles outside Troy's place as he filled in the ruts with barrow loads of tiles and brick rubble. Troy in his turn moaned about Roy's dogs and the jagged debris that damaged his tyres. Like bitter cousins, the two of them hardly spoke. They may have behaved like old enemies but they had only known each other for two years. Time passed slowly. The enmity began during their first summer when a young Canadian woman called Trisha came to the village. Every evening she went to the bar. Roy would chat to her until his head fell down onto the table top. At that point, Troy moved in with his crooked grin and tales of the North Sea fishing boats. Every night he told her about the fantastical contraptions he was making from oil drums so that the next day Trisha talked about nothing else but Troy's machines. This sent Roy into a rage.

'He doesn't need a girlfriend.' He said, 'Not like I do.'

Nothing seemed to work for Roy. If he stayed sober Trisha just thought he was boring. If he got to the bar early, he would be pissed by 7 pm and if he came late, she would already be sitting with Troy. Roy's final attempt was to ask her out on a date. The only problem with his plan was that the date was a funeral.

'Get your glad rags on,' he said. 'Well, I don't mean glad rags of course. What I mean is wear something smart.'

He must have thought it would be an interesting experience and it could have been, under normal circumstances, had he chosen a normal burial.

Kaloyan was an old guy who looked after Dave's sheep and when his wife died, he asked the *Anglichani* to dig the grave. His neighbours refused to help. They did not trust him for, in his youth Kaloyan had killed his own father with a saucepan and then spent 30 years inside for the Freudian crime. I kid you not. Knowing his back story, the police held onto his wife's body for an autopsy and Kaloyan had to arrange everything himself even transporting her from the morgue. By the time they collected the body, the poor woman had started to decompose in the August heat. They took her body from the hospital in a truck with an open back and Roy threw up by the grave side as they tried to lower her down. She was a heavy woman and there were four of them holding the ropes. The British grave diggers were the only people at the burial except for Dobri the Mayor and of course Trisha who had come along in smart clothes borrowed from the woman in the shop, in the hope there would be a decent spread. She ended up holding a scarf across her nose, eyes watering and trying hard not to look shocked. At the bar, around the table that Friday night, Dave told the story with a grim expression on his face.

'Fair play to Dobri. He gave something to pay for the *nekrolog*. From his own money,' Dave said and drained the last of his beer.

Roy groaned with his head flat on the table again, 'Ah Dave, don't remind me man.'

'Why have you still got your tie on? The funeral was two days ago.'

'Wish I could hang myself. I thought it was going to be a free buffet. No one said we had to dig the fuckin' grave.'

I am not sure what happened to Trisha. They say that after that she moved on towards Turkey.

Back in the UK, funerals had always been formal occasions but in the village, there was rarely a priest and never any ceremony. It was left to the elder relatives to lead the mourners. They said a few words and then poured wine on the graves and left bottles of *rakia* on the top of the mound, somewhere close to the position of the head. Kaloyan's wife's funeral was even further removed from what we were used to. He had no social standing and no friends.

It made me think about my own funeral and I am sure that Troy and Roy and all the others did the same. Were they helping Kaloyan because they could see themselves in him? Those single men knew that one day it would be time for their own. Who was going to bury them? Would anyone feel generous enough to waste good booze and pour Jack Daniels onto the grave soil? I watched them all from a distance, detached, amused, without realizing that we had much more in common than I thought.

Our house looked onto the street but at the back, the balcony faced the garden. Here there was nothing but birds, buzzing insects, woodpeckers and butterflies. As the years have passed in Bulgaria I have looked more towards this privacy and nature and shied away from the public façade. These days, I rattle around in the house like a recluse. Once you start declining invitations to bridge nights and barbecues, they dwindle away. People stop asking.

After we had given up the guest house, I looked for work online and savoured the peace and the space and, if I am completely honest, the lack of people. For me, what singles this country out from other places is not the history or the climate but the capacity for isolation. I did not have this in mind when we first arrived. In the early days, we organized parties and gatherings but after a few years things changed. As Claire began to spend more time in Sofia for workshops, I retreated into my writing. So, when the Coronavirus hit and the guidance was to self-isolate, I did not resist. There was no need to wait for the symptoms to develop. I was already showing signs. Lockdown suited me.

I wonder whether this enjoyment of solitude has something to do with childhood. At school we were thrown together in dormitories and classrooms without any personal time. Privacy was impossible. We lived in groups without much love but we survived.

Losing yourself inside a big old house can satisfy competing impulses, one for being seen and the other for staying hidden, both at the same time. The house stands there, visible to the world. There is a public face but it can also promote solitude because when you are inside, it hides you. You can look back to the garden and the flowers and the passing weather and the falling leaves, all day long if you want, without seeing another soul.

I have been in Bulgaria for 12 years and I was at boarding school for 7. My time there was cut short when I was expelled aged 15. Afterwards, I was no longer allowed to mix with the other boys but I still had to take my O'level exams so I sat them alone, supervised by dusty old housemasters, drafted in out of retirement. I did not want their pity so I snarled at them as if they were collaborators. Looking back, I can see that not everyone was against me.

Two months after the O'level exams, in August it was time for me to check the results. I was standing in the main hallway of the deserted school scanning the lists on the noticeboard when a voice came from the doorway. 'C.R.' he said as he held on to the doorframe on one side. It was my Latin teacher, Mr Highley. I looked down at his trainers as he shook my hand. How did I seem to him standing there? Lost? Alone? Expelled with no future? Not at all. He was delighted to see me. More delighted than I had ever known him.

'C.R!' he said again, 'Seeing you has done me more good than jogging ever will.'

Perhaps he liked the quiet places. The empty school corridors, outside of term time, may have suited him. After that, I often saw Mr Highley on the terraces at Boothferry Park watching Hull City, wrapped up in a big coat with his trademark woolly hat on his head, half time thermos in the bag, three quarters of an hour drive from home. And that is pretty much the model I followed too, drawn to honest, unusual people like Mr Highley, like Pokriv, Troy and Cruyff, finding myself at home in the out of the way places. Places like Podgoritsa.

After ten years, the idealism of the early years and our unlimited reserves of energy had faded. We even gave up the guest house and the animals. Was my real motivation behind leaving the UK simply to become a recluse? By then, Ivelina had managed to get a passport for Esme and they had both gone off to work in the UK, so if I ever wanted to catch up on village gossip, I would walk up to Troy's place.

He was squatting on the flat bed to sort out some problem with the gasifier. This was a home-made machine that powered his truck with wood gas instead of petrol. A jet of flame spurted up from one of the smaller drums. Troy blew out the flame for effect and it evaporated into dirty smoke. Then he fired it up again and the flame glowed slightly blue.

'Like the old British town gas. Dirty Old Town and all that,' he said.

'Manchester?'

'I met my love by the gasworks wall.' He sang and then added, 'Salford to be accurate.'

'Dreamed a dream by the old canal,'

'Dirty old town..... Dirty old town.' The two of us sang till we woke the cat.

He told me that all you needed was a fire box and a series of pipes to take the flammable gas to the engine. His home-engineered gas-powered van was the ultimate DIY vehicle and the Bulgarian men in the village loved it. There was even a film crew who came from Sofia to do a piece for breakfast TV on Troy and his machines. That made him into a local celebrity. In Popovo, school kids pointed at him in the street as he chugged past in his home-made car. The rest of us were all jealous of his accidental fame.

'Do you know a pub in Sheffield called the Duck and Chickens?' he said.

Of course. It was notorious. But I had never been inside so I told him about the Bleak House in Walkley where they sold duty free cigarettes under the bar and the Royal Oak with the full-size snooker table, and a landlord who reminded me of Will Self. If I went back there, I would have a pint in each one as if I was on holiday somewhere foreign, ticking off the sites. Maybe I would always feel like a foreigner now, even there. Maybe I always had.

'Well, Matty reckoned that the carry-on last Friday night in the bar, Roy fighting and all that, was better than anything he had ever seen in the Duck and Chickens,' Troy said.

He sat in front of a laptop watching 1970s TV. The old sofa was a rare piece of comfort in a house that felt more like a workshop. It was warm because of the stove. The metal cylinder had a neat welded joint around the top edge and the scraps of wood he fed into the hopper, were consumed immediately in orange flames.

'Just can't get it right. The rocket stove. It burns too quickly then too slow. I tried welding extra boxes and baffles on but it didn't help.'

He stopped to finish rolling a cigarette,

'Might have to go back to old school this winter. Burning massive blocks like the rest of you. So, I am thinking of taking the roof off the house with no documents. Wanna' give me a hand, dude with your chainsaw?'

'Not keen to dismantle a roof,' I said. 'Why don't you ask Dave, then split the wood?'

He handed me the tobacco and the cigarette papers and when I reached over for the lighter I saw Miss Marple on his laptop screen, sitting upright in the back of a London taxi.

'So, what made you come here?' I asked him.

'To be honest buddy. All the shit I had to put up with. Living in the van. The feds were always on my case.'

He took out his laser gun and pointed the red light at the wall of the stove,

'What does it say?'

'405 degrees.'

He took a huge drag as if he was sucking the life out of the rolly,

'Never mind that rocket stove. I can get it going before the cold comes. Just wait till you see the chipper I am building. It's industrial.'

Back in East Yorkshire, there was a village which was not quite a village. It had two big brick farms and a row of cottages built for the farmworkers. The name was Low Gardham to distinguish it from High Gardham which was up on the Wolds about three miles away. Tim Botterill lived in Low Gardham in one of the cottages. When I was a kid in Dalton, he was our family gardener and I remember him burning garden waste behind the old stables, quietly tending the fire, a mound of dry conker leaves with smoke slowly filtering out. There were never any flames because smouldering was the key to burning leaves. His pipe smouldered too, all day long, unless he was on his break, sitting on the stone steps outside the back door tapping the old tobacco out then filling the pipe again from a pouch. If you were lucky, you might walk past just as he opened it and then you would get a whiff of the fresh tobacco, like spicy Ottoman musk, much sweeter than the old wedges of rotten baccy he dropped onto the gravel next to his car.

Tim had his black moods. 'That is why he was single,' my dad said.

'Christopher,' Tim would say to me, never hello or anything like that just my name which was welcome recognition in a family of five. To be fair, he pronounced my name slightly differently with a short 'i' sound in the middle, Christ-i-pher. Mum never allowed him to smoke the pipe in the house so when he was sitting round the kitchen table with his milky tea and biscuits he would lay the pipe out, the bowl cold for once next to his tea cup. I never paid much attention to him when I was young, but I could see he was uncomfortable in that kitchen even though the two of them had long conversations round the table. He was more relaxed when he was outside clipping the roses, raking up leaves from the conker trees and of course standing guard over the bonfires that always seemed to round off the day.

When my mum was dying of cancer, Tim had come to see her and it shocked me to see him with his head in his hands on the steps, fumbling with his pipe. He turned to me with red eyes and his mouth said, 'Christ-i-pher,' but there was no real sound. And that wasn't his only reason for grief.

I knew Tim had two sons a bit younger than me and I also knew that he raised them himself. Mum must have known the whole story about his relationship with their mother but she never shared it. She was not one for gossip. I did not meet the two sons until they were older when the three of them came to live with us.

A year or two later, Tim was struggling. He needed somewhere to live and when the word got back to my dad, he offered him a place. He took over his old job again, pruning roses, mowing the lawn, weeding the beds, raking and burning the leaves. For a few years he was part of the family as we made sense of the future without mum.

One day Tim heard something in the cottage, on the floor which above sounded like a heavy stone.

'Like a stone,' he said.

His son was not ill, it was sudden death. The doctors could not explain what had happened. Tim was never the same after that day when he came running into the house looking wildly about him and telling us to come and see.

I had always wondered what went through his mind as he stared at the smoking leaves. Once I knew he had run upstairs to find his son's body and watched the trolley wheeled out of there, I did not have to wonder any more because I could see the grief in his eyes, red from the smoke and written in his face.

Pokriv, Troy, Tim and Mr Highley were solitary men who kept themselves in. They were personable and creative, good men and often misunderstood. Outsiders. I could do worse than to follow them, to emulate their lack of self regard and natural honesty. As I retreated into our little haven, I realized that I had been visited by these lonely men all my life. They spoke to my tendency for quiet solitude. I never saw myself as a loner and I had Claire to keep me sane and to share our love but I knew that part of me, the social side, was becoming more like them. Should it trouble me to know that? I am not sure.

I could go for weeks without seeing anyone but sometimes we had sociable periods which lasted for days on end when people were coming over every night. It depended on who was in the village. Those party times were like a festive wave that gathered pace out at sea and then crashed onto the shore in a froth of smiling *rakia*. Claire said it had something to do with the phases of the moon.

That particular spree began with Matty's 70th birthday. He was a retired jockey from Doncaster. We had all been drinking *rakia* in the bar since 7 pm and by the end of the evening I was adamant that this was a good time to show them a piece of village history. When I asked Matty a few days later, he said that they were all so sick of hearing about the mysterious 'Communist Museum' that himself and his wife Peggy agreed to come along just to shut me up. Everyone else was looking for somewhere to go drinking after the bar and when I saw Matty and Peggy by the car I beckoned them across the road,

'Why don't we go in now,' I said. 'Then we can catch the rest of them up in a bit. It's just here.'

We slipped in through the metal gate and, using our phones, found the way round the back of the house.

'Quite a place, Chris,' Matty said as we walked through the stone walled cellars with their carved wooden columns,

'Do you reckon it's up for sale?'

On the first floor of the old village museum, abandoned since the early 1990s, I shone my torch on the faces of the local Partisans from 1943, black and white photos of the village men who hid themselves for two years in the forests. The three of us jumped when we heard a noise downstairs. Matty dropped his guitar and the strings vibrated in the empty room.

'I don't think we should have come. Dobri's going to kill me,' I said, suddenly sober.

'Chris? Where are you mate?' came a voice out of the darkness.

'Sounds like Troy,' said Peggy.

'Dude. You there?' Troy appeared in the doorway and we relaxed for a second until he told us that the rest of them were coming. I could see he was scoping the place out for a party, looking into the corners of the rooms with his phone light.

'Definitely not here,' I said.

Roy came in with an Australian couple, about 25 years old who were volunteering with Katie. Roy was wearing an old Pink Floyd T-shirt and carrying a penny whistle.

'I thought you said we had found somewhere. Is this it?' someone said scanning around the ruins of looms in the torchlight.

'How the fuck do I know?' said Roy and slumped down on the floor as Peggy took hold of the Australian girl's arm and helped her back down the stairs,

'Come on love let's get you home.' She said and then I caught Matty's eye and he said,

'You get one arm I'll grab the other,' and we half dragged Roy to the car.

'I've left my penny whistle up there,' he said as we struggled down the stairs.

Troy spoke sharply,

'Forget about that whistle Roy. It's in the museum now. You can leave it there. No one gives a shit anyway.'

15

An English Garden in Sofia

When Hristo came to see us in the house, I showed him the framed picture we had found in the attic space. It was a family group, standing in three rows below the balcony. We knew it must be our house because we recognized the decoration around the window. In the picture, there are five kids in the central row, with three women behind them and two men in front with a sewing machine on a small table. The oldest of the women is holding a hooded Goshawk in her outstretched hand. The men have grand moustaches and hold bottles and tobacco pipes. There is snow on the ground and you can see the freshness of the cold in the cheeks and in the eyes. Hristo thought it must have been taken in the 1930s, in what he called 'bourgeois times,' that is to say, before Communism. They look healthy, as if they must have been well prepared for the winter and Hristo told us that back then, only those with money could have afforded a photograph like this.

Something about such a traditional family scene made Hristo think of Vasil Levski because, like a priest relating Jesus to everyday life, Hristo tended to see Levski in all situations. He could apply the martyr's sayings to any topic. That led him on to talk about an Englishwoman Mercia MacDermot whose book about Levski had the title *The Apostle of Freedom*. He pronounced her surname with stress on the last syllable and I did not recognize the woman's name until he wrote it down on a piece of paper. He told us how he had once seen the authoress herself in Sofia bus station, years before, on an excursion. His school teacher indicated a woman to the class. She was tall and elegant standing there in the crowd, but Hristo could not go and introduce himself like the others because he was nervously trying to keep something hidden under his coat. He and his schoolmates were on their way back from Yugoslavia and he had rashly smuggled a Beatles record across the border. When he got home, he played it secretly on the record player with all the curtains drawn, heart beating, as softly as he could and as loudly as he dared. In 1970 the Beatles were still banned in Bulgaria.

Forty years ago, Mercia MacDermot was a celebrity in Sofia and it seems strange that no streets were ever named after her. When I enquired at the book stalls that used to be on Slaveikov Square they all knew the famous lady's work and one of them rushed off to get a copy from his store room. He explained to me how happy he felt when a foreign scholar like her took an interest in Bulgarian history. The edition he showed me was from 1979 and he held on to it and suggested other titles I might like, as if he did not really want to let it go. I gave him 40 leva in the end. MacDermot must have had a thing about martyrs as she carried a clipping of Levski's hair in a locket around her neck. She also wrote books on Gotse Delchev and Sandansky, both passionate patriots who died for the national ideal, just like Levski.

She was one of the few English people living in Sofia during the 1960s and 1970s and spent seven years teaching at the English School but when she first came to Bulgaria in 1947, she had been one of the international students who helped to build the Koprinka Dam, just outside Kazanluk. The international work brigade was named after an Englishman, Frank Thompson who had been killed only four years before when he was fighting as a British SOE agent with Bulgarian communist partisans. Another Bulgophile product of elite English education. Another martyr. Thompson was a poet of the old school, passionate and earnest, a young man whose idealism placed him somewhere between Lord Byron and TE Lawrence.

Frank Thompson's grave is in Litakovo, close to where he was killed, but in Sofia there is a memorial for him in the English war cemetery. On a bronze plaque raised up slightly from the grass, there is a line from one of his own poems, an epitaph for soldier poets that almost echoes his own death. He wrote it at the age of 20. The BKP made him into a hero and his name lives on in streets and villages dedicated in his honour soon after the end of the war.

There are many connections between the small number of English intellectuals who had contact with Bulgaria in the mid-century decades. Steven Runciman had met Patrick Leigh Fermor in a Sofia hotel and a few years later during the war, Fermor met Frank Thompson in Cairo while both men waited to be posted into action in Europe. Did Frank recognize a kindred literary spirit in Fermor, when in a letter home he calls him, 'a classy captain who eyed the other ranks with disdain.'

Frank exchanged letters with the young Iris Murdoch during the war because they had been students in Oxford together and it was Murdoch who had persuaded him to join the Communist Party of Great Britain (CPGB) in the first place. She never forgot him and in the 1970s she went to Sofia with his brother Edward to take part in a programme about Frank for Bulgarian TV.

Franks's brother Edward was the labour historian EP Thompson, who after the war was part of the CPGB historian's group that also included Chrsitopher Hill and Eric Hobsbawm. Edward was opposed to Stalinism as much as he was to western capitalism and imperialism. The leadership of the CPGB on the other hand, remained loyal to the Soviet Union for far too long. Many British communists ignored the leadership of their party and cancelled their subscriptions as soon as they understood the depth of Stalin's repression or once they heard reports of how the Soviet Union stamped out dissent in Hungary in 1956 and then again in Czechoslovakia in 1968.

In the English corner of the Sofia cemetery most of the dead soldiers were from the First World War. There were also British pilots from the second, shot down over Sofia, during an episode of bombing that has never been forgotten for the damage it inflicted on that sacred capital. I mistook the gardener resting on a gravestone for a visiting relative but he told us that he worked in the garden full time. The lawn was well watered and the grass, green and springy. Between each grave he had planted shrubs and flowers. It was so rare to find a place like this in dusty late summer Sofia, a real oasis. I was almost embarrassed to feel comforted by it, perhaps having become too accustomed to the functionality of that city, and amazed to feel that I wanted to stay for as long as possible in this garden space. It had been preserved for decades in the spirit of quiet forgiveness and common humanity and I wondered if Mercia MacDermot had ever come here in the 1970s to read the names of her compatriots. As we dawdled over Thompson's epitaph poem, I felt sentimental and moved. This took me by surprise. It confused me.

Struck by the cool beauty and unexpected peace, just behind Sofia bus station, for the nostalgia of an English garden the whole thing made me look up one of Thompson's poems, written on his first trip to Crete when he was 18, to dig at Mycenae with Arthur Evans. The next time we sat down with Hristo we talked about Thompson and with his help I tried to translate this line into Bulgarian for him because it meant something to me.

'Here in this land of blue unclouded sky. This languid land of death. I long for home.'

16

Ghosts

With her mother and brother both gone, Krasimira could take no comfort. As far as she was concerned, she was on her own. Nobody else was living through the same deep sadness so as soon as the doctor confirmed she had cancer, even when she could still work in the garden, she began to talk openly about dying. We stopped saying things like, 'Don't be talking like that, you have many more years yet,' because we knew she didn't. It was a fate she shared with the whole village. Everyone accepted their mortality. A few stubborn survivors stared back aggressively when death appeared, but most people were forever glancing behind them, as if the figure of mortality were following along the street. As soon as they fell ill, they were quick to accept the coming end.

And die she did. It was the year of Covid 19 lockdown and the Bulgarian health service was under resourced and over stretched and many doctors and nurses had themselves died from the virus. I was in a two-week quarantine, in isolation inside the house and I heard the cars pulling up next door and all the people arriving for the wake. This time I could not attend. I listened to the chimes of the village bell emitting its ghostly vibes across the rooftops, especially for her, and wondered whose job it was to pull the rope now that Ivan the bell ringer had also succumbed?

Inactive under quarantine, I slept all day and during those deep daytime naps, I left my body. There was so much space in Podgoritsa, even in dreams. The acres of trees and the airy freedom of the breeze made the dreamscape more expansive, filling my head with distortion. The stories sprang from an old shoe cleaning box which had sat for years on the flagstones in the back hall at Dalton, in the house where I grew up. Now it was in our shed in Podgoritsa. How could I forget the brushes with their stiff bristles for putting on polish and the softer ones for bringing up a shine. I had left Dalton at 16 because it was too boring but now it came to life again. In quarantine dreams.

I could see the faded colours of that English village, a place in my memory where each of the estate cottages on Main Street had a front step made of grit stone. From here the snicket led through the yew trees to our house. I walked up again from the bus stop and the pigeons flapped about in the high branches, right next to the grave yard. I climbed over the low wall and read the East Riding surnames on the head stones: Roebuck, Griffin, Dilcock.

These memories of Dalton are beautiful ones especially the details: The moss on the gravestones that, in summer peeled off in a whiff of dust or, in wet weather came away from the incised names as a thick bed of roots; The coloured glass and gravel on the graves or the small red fruits of the yew tree, inedible like drops of blood.

Back in the summer of 1974, the nave of the church was cool and deserted and I never dared touch the bell rope in case it sucked me up inside that forbidding spire. During the last summer before boarding school, I wasted time gaping at Baronet Hotham's tomb. It was pure Renaissance Gothic from 1689. The tomb had two levels. The reclining figure of the baronet clad in riding gear and leather gloves with a marble skeleton below. Both of them were life size. In the church, the tall arch between the nave and chancel read,

'I was glad when they said unto me, let us go into the house of the lord.'

Those words meant nothing to me at all, even though I had sat in those pews and read the Victorian inscription a thousand times. At the end of the summer, we went off to Hull to buy a school uniform and mum sewed the name tags into every item, *C. R. Fenton 212*, each one like her own small spell. She packed my trunk and then on the final day we lifted it out to the car. I sat on the shoe cleaning box by the back door and waited to leave. I can barely remember that day, but from then on nothing was going to be the same. I was eight years old and my shoes were perfectly clean.

We were so privileged in many ways. They gave us an elite education but it was also a curse because it denied us some basic luxuries. There was no family life and no love. For 8 year old kids, if this is not direct abuse, it could surely be seen as neglect. We went home on certain special Sundays that they designated as 'leave out'. Dalton was only 20 minutes from school and I think that is why Sunday, especially in the Autumn as the light fades early, has a mournful quality still because I remember how it felt, late on Sunday afternoon, to leave behind our conkers and bikes and get into the car and go back to the boarding house. Saying goodbye to the house in Dalton with its perfumed garden, whose fragrance was so delicious that I knew it could never last.

Walking alone down the lanes of Dalton as a child, or trespassing secretly in the woods I always felt I was with someone else. In the village dump I threw stones down at the broken cars and fridges and later I hid packs of Benson and Hedges cigarettes behind a loose brick in the walled garden. I was with a kind of friend, someone with a conscience exactly like my own. Sometimes he was a pure mirror, but otherwise, a lens that could sharpen ideas and apply them to the world. We walked together for hours. I found him too on mountain tops and in the sea caves of Argyll.

I wander the forests and fields of Bulgaria in the same company and when I graze the goats in abandoned gardens, he is there with me for sure. I wonder whether it used to be my adult self and now it is my child self but there is absolutely no face or shape or sound. This was the ghost I knew best.

In Dalton I don't remember seeing others. The magical spaces of that landscape, from the medieval stories and place-names had already been taken away by Enclosure, financed and designed by the Baronet's great grandson. When his surveyors fenced off the commons, they un-stitched the names and re-routed the roads. Once the village peasants stopped going to the fields, the ghosts and spirits must have left, as if it had been the constant human passage, the speaking out loud of stories and names that kept them alive. In Bulgaria this had not happened, the landscape was still active and once I had the time to walk around on my own, the ghosts started to show themselves.

When peace returned to Podgoritsa after the 1877-8 war, the mothers of the dead Russian Cossacks made the long journey to the village to see their graves. Now they were back. Nobody knew exactly how long the Russian mothers had been around, behind the glass-less windows, re-arranging things, hammering on the walls and getting ready for a long stay. After some days they spread out across the village and mingled with the residents but everyone could see they did not belong.

The people were concerned. They talked about them in the post office queue and when they gathered around the *petchka* in the big shop,

'Have they bought any wood?'

'Do they have *burkani*?'

'I could lend a mincer.'

Winter was coming and the Russian mothers were not doing anything to get ready. They just kept on searching for their sons. When Dobri the mayor showed them the old museum they saw the picture of the mass grave where their boys had lain for 143 years. The garden of the house where they were squatting was completely overgrown and they had no animals, not even rabbits or chickens. Everyone was worried about them.

'What will they do when the snow comes? The oldest one has only very light shoes. I never see her in anything waterproof,' said Margarita (Milk and Honey).

In the cold weather we had to wait for the frost to melt before the goats could go in the morning. Frozen dew cast itself over the garden like a veil. I was stamping my feet in the thin sunlight when Yuliana walked up with an armful of sticks. Her mother was born in the 1920s, and the 90-year-old remembered being told that these women had left jewellery and gold to pay for a chapel out in the fields in memory of their sons. She also knew that Baba Yordanova had gone to the chapel every day to light a candle because her own baba had gone with her. As a young girl, she had walked up there with the older woman on every single visit to the chapel, all those years before in the 1880s and 1890s.

The Russian mothers had paid Baba Yordanova and the family kept the gold ring for decades, but after Yordanova died, the chapel was forgotten and the ring cashed in. Nobody remembered the chapel and even Yuliana's mother did not know the place where it once stood. A few years ago, I had a poke about in a clump of trees in the middle of the arable and there were piles of stone and roof tiles in there. That spot would have been a good site for the chapel because it was on the actual battlefield and just up the hill from the mass grave. Maybe that was the place but nobody remembered any more, not even Hristo knew for sure.

On the anniversary of the battle, they went to check on the visitors but no one could find them in the house. The small group could hardly open the door, swollen as it was from years of heat and damp. Stefka, Margarita (Milk and Honey) and the mayoral secretary searched other places like the bus shelter and the church. When it started to rain like it always did in Autumn, big drops heavy and cold, the three of them just went home.

Yuliana said that tomorrow there would be a service in the church to remember the Russian boys. She had bought some fish because if you eat fish on *Nikulden*, the feast of St Nicholas, you will be healthy for the whole year. The church was an open hall with chairs lined up along two walls. The *petchka* was an oil drum with a battered flue that ran up to the ceiling. It turned in mid-air, high up in the space and went out through a hole in the wall. Dunka came in with an armful of sawn planks and fed them into the fire making the whole contraption rattle as the flames took hold. The priest was restless, walking backwards and forwards, coming out from behind the *ikonostas* to see who had come in.

Claire and I sat down next to Violeta and when she introduced us, the priest shook our hands and held onto them with his freezing cold fingers. Then he walked away and started to sing. He opened the central doors so we could hear him clearly all through the church even when he was behind the screen. He sang in deep vowels which echoed forever and I wondered about the Russian mothers who had lit candles here and thought that they must have said prayers in this very church.

When the people came in, they went over to the icon stand. In boots and ski jackets from the Popovo second hand shops, they crossed themselves and kissed the image of St Nicholas. The priest continued to sing, praising the village and the animals and the country and the government and everyone who had died. On and on he went.

Sometimes a mobile phone rang but it was no big deal. After the priest had included everyone's name in the prayers, he seemed to suddenly remember the food and then he waved the incense over the mackerel, two candles stuck in the flesh like a birthday cake. There was a loaf of bread in a plastic packet and a Pepsi bottle filled with red wine. He intoned over the food and then, with his wooden cross in one hand, he dipped the posy of dried herbs into the holy water and sent the droplets flying. Each one of us received a shower. Violeta told me later that it was not something she had witnessed as a child, this kind of blessing, because she was born in 1947 and her youth had been under Communism when the church was closed. She came back to these things later in life because she knew that it was something her parents had done before the 9 September 1944, and it was something that they had missed for her and it seemed kind of natural now to revive the tradition.

Winter days were short. As I waited for the goats on that December afternoon the moon was a full white force in the sky. With magic, it charged what was left of the day. Petar had climbed the acacia tree for a better view. He was up there in the lower branches watching the moon rise over Sune's roof saying,

'Wash him, wash him. That will not help. Washing the face won't make any difference to what's inside his head. It's just a waste of soap and water.'

The cows went past and after them the smell of new potatoes and mint. Petar took out a box of matches from his pocket and shook them at me. Maybe he knew what was coming.

The sky brightened above the hill to reveal a moon-lit space. I could see to the back of the sky room and there they were, the Russian mothers with white skin and black shawls clapping home their wounded sons in a line. In those Slavic women, I could see my neighbours, Krasimira, Simona, Ivelina and Violeta. Reflected in their eyes were the faces of the sons, brothers and fathers they had lost, as if the stories from the cold battlefield, the perceived glory and nobility of loss, had coloured the grief consciousness of the village for every generation since 1877.

In Dalton, most of the men were as ancient as the place. Fothergill's garden smelt of mown grass and Frank Bell kept ferrets in cages at the back of his house. These guys had worked all their lives on the Hotham Estate and they lived out their retirement rent free in the tied cottages. In Podgoritsa, the politics were different but the old people had that same sense of lost belonging, of once having lived in a society that took care of their needs. It was there in both villages. For all these men and women born in the 1930s and 1940s, their experience after 1990 was like living in a world they were not tuned for. The two regimes were all they had ever known and their memories were buried in the ruins. I wondered whether it was the faces of those East Yorkshire men that I saw in the Stefans and the Ivans. Is that what spoke to me of belonging in that Bulgarian village because there were so many echoes of the place where I had grown up?

I slept throughout the long days of quarantine so that after dark I was awake to wander through the rooms of the house and explore the sheds and barns by moonlight. Stepping down from the hay loft was risky. The ladder itself could be as strong as anything, but if it slipped at the bottom on the flagstones, there was nothing you could do, except let yourself go limp and use your arms to protect your head. I smelt the tobacco smoke and heard the old man, telling me to watch out in Bulgarian. '*Vnimanie!*' he would say.

In the hay loft I had to go carefully to avoid the A-frames that held up the roof. They were immoveable beasts of oak and when I banged my head on one of the timbers, I had to stop for a minute to concentrate on coming back down to earth. It was then, head spinning, that I heard the scraping, then the hammer tapping, faster and faster and the final blow at the end. Like music. And the men's voices,

'Come down, I have *tyutyun*.' The word itself sounded like puffing life into a pipe. He was talking about tobacco.

'Wait and we can get more tiles.'

'We can share it.'

'After this one. Is it yours?'

'No. I got it from a Turkish sailor.'

And then suddenly, Belcho barked from down below in the yard and I jumped off the bale and hit my head a second time on the beam, 'Fuck, sorry,' I said but the two men had already gone.

The next time I was in the roof space, I sat on the big beam and swung my legs over the bales sniffing in the warm hay and going dizzy, a bit tipsy on the idea of summer. From certain angles there were chinks of light through the tiles that caught the tiny leaves of *lutserna*. They always said that these barn roofs were more secure than the houses. I heard voices go past on the street. Then a noise close behind made me jump up but this time my head missed the beam. There was a shape lying in the hay, waking up and stretching himself. At first, I thought it must be Petar and that he could be hungover again.

'*Izvinyavam se*. My sincere apologies,' the man said, 'At this age, I have to catch a sleep whenever I can.'

What little light there was, found his black pupils, tiny dark holes against the whites of his eyes. He stirred and moved amongst the bales and brought himself up on his elbows, un-furling his legs. He had a rough bald head with a large moustache and he felt around for his hat and put it back on before he said any more. It was coarse black material and fitted well, over the scalp.

Some of the words were lost, '*Ivan se kazvam*,' and then again as if to make sure I understood, '*Ivan sum.*' His whole body was wrapped in material, legs, arms and waist. He left pauses between the things he said and grunted as he shifted about,

'What animals do you have?' he asked.

I looked at him blankly and he repeated it more slowly.

'Errr, Pigs, chickens, goats. Mainly goats. Only three,' I said in careful clean Bulgarian.

'You don't need more.'

'What about you?' I asked him stupidly.

'These days just the horse and a donkey. *Magare.*'

Then another pause, as he shifted on the hay. It looked like his legs were giving him pain.

'Show me your hands,' he said.

I did not want to go any closer.

'Your hands.'

His fingers were like knotted wood. I held out my own towards him. We reached forward, both of us until his finger-tips met mine. My long slender fingers.

'Just like pig fat,' he said, 'do you play piano? Are you a priest?'

'Violin,' I stuttered.

'I have the hands of a singer.' He laughed at his own joke and rooted around in the folds of his clothes. 'I am going back up to smoke,'

He fumbled at the edges of the pouch with his right thumb where the nail had come off and the skin was calloused up, like a welded joint. And then he was gone and all I could see were the bales stacked up and then I remembered the work of it, heaving them up the ladder and sweating in the heat. My head swimming and my legs weak again from the thought.

I forgot all about him until the next time that I had to go up there for a bale. I heard voices again, this time from men on the roof.

'When Maria came back with the flowers, they had already closed it.'

'Buried?'

'No just put the lid on.'

'What flowers did they use?'

'They filled the coffin entirely with *lutserna* and added mud bricks for the weight and they laid the flowers and leaves of American tobacco on top.'

The silence between the words was like rushing water. Then one of them spoke again,

'He did like a smoke.'

'I still cannot believe it.'

'I am expecting him to walk into the shop.'

'Drowned in the cold sea.'

'That is exactly what they are going to write on his *necrolog.*'

The bell rang on the day of every death, and as it tolled across the village it opened up the gaps between the living and the dead so that on those evenings between death and funeral, the ghosts came out from the overgrown fields and the empty cellars and the broken houses. At the festivals too on the special days when they remembered them with new posters, they welcomed back the dead into the living world. After 40 days, 90 days, one year, five years, ten years. Loving memory down corridors of time. Fading grief like radioactive decay.

Weeks later, freed from my quarantine, I was out on the stubble in the early evening after the animals had wandered home, a week before the ploughing. The goats and sheep and cows of the village had free rein to graze the massive field, picking at the cut stalks, stuffing their mouths with straw. Bird song echoed violently then silence hung over the battle field like a heavy fog. Autumn had set in and the ground was wet. The evenings were much darker than before and the mornings chilled and busy as everybody made their final preparations.

That day, as it got dark, the hill lost its scale but I could still see the shape. The top was rounded like the heel of an upturned foot. The dark lines of bushes and trees ringed the hill like the beard on a mussel. I watched as it moved. The curving line of fringe was an eyelash, the bulge above it, the closed lid of an eye. Sealed by paddocks and field tracks. Closed for centuries. The eyelash was stuck to the skin with age but then it flickered and twitched and broke open, ripping out roots and tearing up the rocky screes of the ditch-sides and showering mud and stones. There was the bright flash of an eyeball as it blinked enormously. Then the eye opened up and I saw the brown iris and livid pupil darting about to see the sky. Trees and soil and grasses like dried snot were gumming the eye's wet film so it blinked and flicked them away with no effort.

And the next day, I was out again, too late for the shepherds. The eyelid was blinking but it soon closed and then the lash kept lifting a little to show the eyes glistening film. To one side, next to the corner, a column of figures came out from behind a tree and made their way in procession along the broken hedge, lifting up the edge of the landscape and tucking in the eye lash under the grassy rim. All the dead heroes walked in silhouette against the darkening sky like tears. The Russian Cossacks, those young men so loved by their mothers, Mara Taseva the partisan, wearing her gallows rope like a necklace, all the bourgeoisie executed by the Popovo People's Court, medals stuffed in their mouths, the chicken sacrificed for the royal meal, Baba Gabriela with folded hands and Mona Lisa smile, Krasimira smoking three cigarettes with Bogdan her brother, all the goat kids I had ever killed with their throats open, Wally the dog, Pokriv with his empty stomach awash with milk, English Rik throwing whiskey bottles across the hillside and old Pesho, taller than all of them with his *gadulka* and little paper cup of coffee and tiny plastic stirrer. They knew what they were supposed to do. They closed the eye for another day and then disappeared again back into the ground out of sight. Winter had come at last. Ready or not.

17

The Winter Walnut Club

Simona and Violeta had spent nine months preparing so as soon as the snow came, they stopped work immediately and began their hibernation beside the *petchka*. Winter was like a long sleep. It was the closest thing to actual death, other than death itself.

Violeta's curved metal hook was useful for many jobs but not this one. Her hair looked wild under the scarf and she stooped forward in a medieval silhouette against the grey black sky, trying to drag something down the lane. Claire was on her way to India but I was staying for the winter. The taxi from Bucharest had just dropped me off at home and my bags were lined up outside the gate. It was 5 January and the big snow was on its way.

'Chris will help us but first he needs to change out of those good clothes,' said Simona who had cut her finger chopping onions. I groped at the hay feeder, searching for something to hold between the cold wet metal struts.

'What we need is a sledge,' I said hopefully. Simona clicked her teeth as the gloom of winter fell over her face. Then she remembered the warm kitchen. She smiled sweetly and excused herself from this dirty work by waving the bandaged finger in the air like a flag.

The snow that fell that night did not melt for two months. Every few days, the municipal tractor rumbled along the street to pile it up on the roadside and our useless car disappeared under a mound of white. I dug my way through to the animal yard and twice a day crunched down the tunnel, its sides smooth like a bob sleigh run. The goats and the pig were happy to stay inside but the chickens would venture out to peck in vain at the hard ground. Their drinking water was frozen solid every morning and by the end of February there were at least 20 bucket-shaped blocks of ice scattered across the yards. Warm in the house, with time on my hands, I read famous winter stories and watched winter films; *Independent People* by Laxness and *Dr. Zhivago* with Omar Sharif and Julie Christie. I told myself that I would survive, knowing my situation was not quite so full of jeopardy as theirs. Nonetheless, there was plenty of drama to come before the Spring.

At some time in the middle of January, a whole ham disappeared from the porch, so I ventured out to repair the fence, following the yellow dog piss holes and pawprints in the snow like an arctic tracker. The street dogs had left other signs. Flattened snow, fluffy hair stuck on the wire and a slipper stolen from the house. I did my best to fix the fence but now that the ground level was a metre higher than before, the dogs were jumping over. The forgetful snow had buried all traces of the other place, the summer paths and flower beds. Stuck in the limbo of winter, I could not go forward and I could not go back. The past was frozen under my feet and the future too, remote and impossible to imagine.

Then everything changed. Somebody pushed a flyer under the front door. The paper was dry, in spite of the snow that was everywhere. Walter had delivered a personal invitation. In capitals, he wrote,

WINTER WALNUT CLUB! MEN ONLY. NO
PARTNERS.
Come for the crack! Just bring walnuts.

I was not sure about getting involved, especially in the winter when venturing out at night was a major expedition but Claire was away in Kerala and the snow showed no signs of melting. I decided to give it a go.

There were five of us at the first meeting, Sune, Troy, Antony, Walter and myself. I looked across the table at their red cheek faces and it seemed like we could have been Victorian explorers, marooned together on some icebound vessel. At the second gathering Walter spent a long time telling us about his childhood home in Surrey and it quickly became confessional as he recounted his father's winter punishments. Sune spoke of a farm in Sweden where the snow banked up against the windows and I did my bit by telling the boys about Dalton as we passed around the nutcracker and shared the bowl for the broken shells. They all laughed at me and said my childhood was tame by comparison with theirs.

The house we lived in as kids, I told them, the one we saw in the school holidays, was old and rambling with an endless garden where we could wander for hours. I loved the approach from the road. As we passed the old mere there was an entrance to a hidden driveway and then, as the car rounded the corner, tyres crunching on gravel, the view of the house opened up. I remember one time at school when the teacher asked us to draw our home so I painted a big Georgian place, filling the page with rows of rectangular windows on two floors, and Mr. Loney hated it and told me not to be so ridiculous. He wanted a more standard image, two windows upstairs two down, door in the middle, chimney on top with smoke and a garden path.

'But my house doesn't look like that,' I said and he mistook my honesty for arrogance.

I was nine years old when he first beat me with a training shoe for some misdemeanour. He struck with vengeance. I could feel it, and afterwards, I saw with some clarity, when all my senses were on fire, that he had hurt his own wrist. If that was the worst they could do, I was going to be invincible.

Winter in the Dalton house could be draughty and cold. The high ceilings and sash windows made it difficult to heat. Open fireplaces warmed the downstairs rooms and I learned at an early age to clean out the grates and lay the fires. First you had to scrunch newspaper into balls, select the driest kindling then the bigger pieces of wood and finally, carefully put the coal chunks on top, one by one. Paper, wood and coal had to be in perfect balance or else the fire would not catch. By the age of ten I was an expert. Forty years later, during that cold Bulgarian winter, I put the life skill into good use feeding the *petchka* during the night so there would still be a few red embers glowing in the morning below the surface of grey ash.

At the club meetings, we sat around an old dining table in Walter's kitchen. It was a family heirloom and over 100 years old. He allocated the four of us to our places as if it were a dinner party but the chairs at the two heads, he left empty. Most of the time, we concentrated on cracking the hard nuts and then breaking apart the shells and picking out the fractured pieces of soft walnut. I assumed he left the chairs free to maintain the intimacy or maybe even the equality of the group but I was wrong about that. Nobody talked much, as we cherished the rare feeling of shared company, hands busy, jaws moving slowly, chewing, chewing. We washed them down with whiskey as a plastic Chinese clock pinged every 15 minutes. That tinny digital sound reminded us that time was passing and every few minutes we reached over for another nut. The peace was usually broken by Troy who hated being quiet so he would say something obvious to do with the weather. Sune and I were happy to stay silent. The polished wooden table-top shone like obsidian glass and the Swede was always looking down so he could see his own bearded face in there, a blurry reflection that mirrored his actual view of the world, as the evening progressed and the whiskey went down.

Walter's cat was prowling around under the table and it had chosen Troy's legs as a kind of ladder, digging its claws through his trousers and long johns.

'Get that cat off me Walt,' said Troy.

'Zalmoxis. Leave the nice man alone,' said Walter, 'and go back to your den.' The cat slunk off. It was a sleek Persian with long legs and narrow eyes and its arrogant look un-nerved us all.

'Listen everyone. Can you use the coasters? I don't want any marks,' said Walter, 'and please do not call me Walt.'

Troy whispered, 'This is like being back at school.'

Then he shouted out, 'Walter why do you call the cat such a stupid name?'

'Because I believe her to be immortal. I have lost count of that beast's age. When I inherited her, she was already very old but that was 25 years ago. Zalmoxis was an ancient deity, Thracian I believe. From these parts.'

Having lived close to the Arctic Circle, Sune must have known something about winter but walnuts were new, at least to have them in such abundance. He only spoke when he had something important to share.

'I am a bit like that,' he said.

Walter got up and filled our glasses. The four of us listened.

'Like the cat, I have forgotten how old I am or even when is my birthday. Honestly, I do not know. I cannot remember. I could be 85 but then again, I might yet be over 100.'

Then he raised his glass,

'A toast please. *Skal*! Cheers! *Nazdrave*! To the immortals.'

'What's your secret?' Antony asked. 'I could do with some.'

'My secret is to stop counting.'

Troy looked dubious. 'Easier said than done.'

The clock ticked on and we fell silent.

Walter sat down deliberately and looked around, picking a dog hair from his fleece, before he made an announcement,

'I propose we leave two empty chairs for our dear departed friends, Rik and Thompson.'

Sune raised the long handle of the nut cracker in agreement as the cat jumped up from Troy's lap onto one of the free chairs and settled herself down. This announcement changed the whole atmosphere. Two ghosts had joined us. Troy looked over to me and opened his eyes wide but said nothing. Thompson and Rik had been life-long friends from Basildon. Now they were buried alongside each other in Podgoritsa graveyard. Maybe they had always had a deathwish even 20 years before when they bought adjacent Bulgarian houses on the internet at the end of a two-day bender. When he showed us the X-Ray, Thompson said that the shadow over his lung on the photo was caused by the extra pack of fags he kept in his top pocket. Then he laughed so much he had a coughing fit that made his eyes water. That was a few weeks before he died. Rik's death was a little more hivernal.

We could all see that Antony was un-settled by the announcement. He had been close to these two and he even knew them vaguely from Essex, but a year or so before they died, there was a row about some car parts for Rik's Mercedes and they hardly spoke after that. Troy put on his Trilby hat and pushed it back over the black stubble on the top of his head. He turned to Sune and changed the subject,

'Did someone take the roof off the house next door to you?' he asked.

'Yah. I did it for the beams,' Sune said, 'hard wood.'

'I had my eye on that one. I was gonna ask you.'

'What about yourself?'

'Left it a bit late but once I get Rik's pile in, I'll be sorted,' said Troy. 'Me and Dave cut up a load of beams at his place before the old piss-head died.'

They both looked up to the ceiling and then drank their whiskey, nodding to one end of the table as a tribute to Rik.

'You better get it in then.'

'Yeah, I know. Don't wanna end up like him.'

The talk of wood made us all think of the fire and Sune got up and loaded another log into the *petchka*. After that the silence came back and my thoughts turned to mortality and our advancing years.

'So what would you do if you got sick?' I said to Troy eventually. 'Would you go back?'

'Fuck that. Back to waiting five hours in A and E? When your time has come it's come, nothing you can do. No point delaying the inevitable.'

He meant it. He would stay by the stove, drink *rakia* and fall asleep as quickly as he could, just like Rik and Thompson had done. And maybe that was why these men were attracted to a village like this, where the dead looked out from every door and where the death bell rang from the tower, calling souls to that other place not so many metres down.

During that winter, any moisture at all was taken away by the cold. The ice crystals on the fence posts were like tiny diamonds. At the start of February, as if tired of hibernation, the hungry pine martens, *belkite* came out and danced over the snow. Sometimes I saw bones and discarded shoes on the white-covered roads and the loose dogs were yellow-eyed and crazy. Gutter pipes reached the ground as frozen waterfalls in strange aqueous formations and long icicles hung down from the roofs.

Most people stayed by the *petchka* and watched TV, slowly working through their jars but once or twice Dobri the Mayor called the men out for an emergency, *avariya*.

On a bright day, there was a whole crowd standing inside the big shop, their boots making pools of meltwater on the tiled floor. The men were going round the houses looking for water leaks and checking on the old folk. I nodded at Hristo and Ivan and the dancing grandson and Meladin and Hrasim from up the top. Ivailo the well digger helped himself to a small bottle of whiskey and poured it into his coffee. Stefka grunted and wrote something down on his tab. They were not allowed to smoke inside the shop but still they tried it and Stefka kept sending them out. Some had shaggy fur coats like horseback warriors, real Bulgarians. Dobri asked me about the Walnut Club and specifically, whether we would take any more members. He said he could spread the word. I told him it was just something we did on special occasions and he seemed satisfied with that and went away to organise the team.

Dobri turned back and asked if I had seen Antony because he knew that he was good at breaking into locked houses. When he arrived, red-eyed, there was a murmur and somebody handed him a plastic cup of whiskey, two full shots. When he looked around at the faces, they all said 'Wheeskee' because they knew he needed fortifying. This time last year the same group had gone round checking, and when Antony broke open the lock he found Rik dead in the barn, his body frozen solid in an old armchair. Rik had sat himself down so he could watch the night sky and gaze at the blurred winter stars. He never woke up. They waited for Rik's son to come out because he wanted to take his dad's body back to Basildon for a proper family funeral but everyone said it was too much trouble with all the forms to fill in and the permissions to get so, in the end they buried him in the village next to Thompson, his old mate from home. The Walnut Club had become a weekly memorial for the two of them.

We passed around the nutcrackers and ate the nuts in silence again until Troy spoke up.

'Is it worth it?

'What?'

'All this effort just for a few scraps of walnut. What's the point?'

'Hold on. We are not doing this for food. That would be sad. We are trying to ease the boredom,' said Walter.

'Ease the boredom? Why not choose something less boring then?'

'Ok. Ease the solitude.'

The clock ticked on. The men shuffled and rustled. Nobody went out for a smoke because it was too cold so Sune shared round the snuff which he took instead of tobacco.

The fire flickered and crackled behind the glass. The cat stretched its immortal legs. Walter kept on adding logs, hard oak and acacia from rescued roof beams. Some of the pieces had metal fittings and nails so in the morning when he cleaned the grate the ash would be full of cold clasps and fixtures that he stored in a bucket and took to the scrap dealer once a year. The hours passed until it was time for us all to go home, crunching off through the snow in the moonlit cold, back to our own ashy fires where we hoped the embers would still be glowing so we could coax the flames back and get it burning again, muttering spells to make sure there would still be some life below the grey ash in the morning not so many hours away.

That night I watched my own fire and thought about Troy's words,

'Don't wanna end up like Rik, do I?'

Rik had not died from a lack of wood but because he had fallen asleep totally drunk in a chair in the unheated barn and, even though he was wrapped in a blanket, had frozen to death. 'Like a fool' we all agreed when we first heard the news but it made us realise how dangerous the winter could be. If you took your eye off the ball. The jeopardy of living alone with addictions. A good supply of wood was a matter of life and death.

Troy did not like spending money so he salvaged his wood from old houses, but this year his plans had not worked out. He came to the next meeting in fur-lined overalls and sat down, a pink wooly hat on his head. He did not look happy.

'I just wanna warm up,' he said.

'We're only two minutes from your place,' said Sune.

'No man, my house is freezing, like a hospital morgue. I went to get all that roof wood from Rik's but it's gone.'

Then he leaned over and grabbed Walter by the arm, 'is it true Walt?'

'What are you talking about?'

'My wood,' he pointed over to the *petchka*, 'Rik gave it to me in his will.'

'The will that he wrote on a fag packet? It was hardly legally binding.'

'That was his will. Everyone agreed. You saw it. It was a proper occasion and he left that wood to me. Dave will vouch for it too. He told me that you collected it from Rik's place two days ago.'

'Well yes, but I paid for it.'

Troy jumped up and let out a scream, waving the nutcracker across the table,

'It's my only wood. You know that. Do you want me to end up like Rik?'

'Dave sold it to him.' said Sune.

'Is that true?'

Walter nodded.

'Fuck this shit.' Troy drank his whiskey. Messily.

'Where you going man?' Sune said, trying to calm him down.

'To Dave's fuckin place.'

'Oh fuckin dear,' said Sune and did another pinch of snuff.

In the silence that followed Walter got up from the table and went over to his cat and gave it a stroke on the top of its head. Not something he usually did but he was uneasy.

When he came back to the table, I asked, 'Did you really buy it?'

'Well yes. Security of supply. And all that.'

'I can't believe you.'

'He'll be ok. He's just being dramatic. That tiny room he lives in. You could heat it with a candle. He can always use the rocket stove.'

'Of course. The rocket stove that doesn't work,' I said.

Staying there any longer would have made me feel like a collaborator so I picked up my things and popped in a final nut and put on my gloves and hat and went out into the snow. The fire was still going when I got home.

I could easily have been on the beach in Kerala with Claire but I had chosen to stay in the village. I knew that a Bulgarian winter was a beautiful thing. It was always going to be safe enough but the cold crept in through the windows and in the morning, the freezing air left etchings of ice on the inside of the glass. All wrapped up in bed, I read *The*

Lion the Witch and the Wardrobe, where the Narnia winter had descended on the land like tyranny and I recognized the comfort in Mr Tumnus' cozy little house and ultimately the hope when the thaw came. Hope for the whole world.

The next day was clear and bright and the sunlight on the snow made my eyes ache. I walked up to check on Troy.

'Frank Zappa. Such a cool genius,' he said, on his second *rakia* of the morning sitting in an armchair surrounded by remote controls and ashtrays. I had my back to the stove, wondering how he got the thing so hot and telling myself I should not drink more than two glasses.

'And these days?' I asked him.

'All the musicians are idiots. The really clever ones make music for computer games.'

'Did you see Dave?'

'Nah. He escaped. Got on a plane yesterday,' said Troy, 'probably used that money he got for the wood. Good job for him. Better for his health all round.'

'What you gonna do?'

He passed me the bottle and picked up his laser thermometer and shone the red light against the cast iron side of the rocket stove.

'See that? I got it to work. Just needed a separate chamber in the fire box. Scraps and shavings. All those forests that you lot decimate to keep your palaces warm over winter. No need for it. Not anymore. All you have to do is clear the verges and turn the twigs into tinder. You could live like that forever.'

A few days later on 3 March, it was all over. The temperature rose dramatically. Ten degrees in a single night. The first morning when I did not need to light the *petchka* was like a new kind of freedom. The fire ash stayed cold all through the day. I parted the tables to clean underneath and saw Walter's flyer down there with the words, 'just bring walnuts.' It already seemed like ancient history. With the thaw, the juice was up. I was alive again. Here came the smells and sounds and the Drip! Drip! Drip! of the snow melting from the roof. The Spring had brought the rain and I could see the ground again but still I missed the sweet melancholia of winter in Narnia. The non-time.

The birdsong returned with the ratter tat of the woodpeckers, their flashes of colour loud against the muck and dirt. I followed the old tracks hidden under the snow for so many months. Life came back with the chainsaws and the revving cars but had anything really changed? I knew we were still going round in circles; longing for the heat of summer, dazzled by the light of the sun, exhausted by August, desperate for the rain to come back, then crying again when the beauty of summer finally faded.

Claire timed her return well and once she was back from India, we decided to do something about Zalmoxis. Not Walter's Persian cat but the real god. The Prince himself.

Zalmoxis was even older than Zeus. According to Herodotus, he was sacred to the Getae, the Thracian tribe who had lived around here on both sides of the Danube and they were interested in immortality. The tombs of Sboryanovo in the heart of Getic territory, were laid out like a constellation, mapped onto the surface of the earth. Some of the Greek sources said Zalmoxis had been a student of Pythagoras, a follower of Orpheus. He had returned to his native Thrace to spend three years in the holy mountain of Kogaion in an underground chamber before re-appearing to his followers, resurrected.

What Walter did not know was that the real Zalmoxis lived in our garden. The immortal one had been sealed up in the mud brick wall for some years and when we dismantled it, we found the signs. We collected all the ornaments, having thought it must have been some kind of shrine. There were offerings of rusted blades wrapped in disintegrating cloths and ribbons stuffed between the bricks, some of them still with their colours bright, unfaded like a miracle. In the wall, we installed a cute little niche so that the mini god had somewhere comfortable to stay. Instead he spent most of the time in the rafters of the barn where he irritated the guests as they did their meditations. Zalmoxis liked to sleep and to encourage him to stay quiet, we made him a bed in an old ammunition box and lined it with straw.

We wanted him out of there so to avoid another year of mischief we grabbed the box, fixed the lid down with nails and carried it to the car. It was light, as if there was nothing inside. We drove to Sveshtari to see the Thracian tomb.

'You'll never get him in there,' Claire said on the way, 'it's all so sanitized.'

The guide asked if I was from Germany so I told her about the guest house and she joked that we would soon need a visa to visit the tomb because the UK was proposing to withdraw from UNESCO. Sveshtari was a World Heritage site, one of seven in Bulgaria.

Claire whispered, 'They're not going let you take that box inside, even with the god in it.'

I wondered whether, during her time in India, she had become used to handling deities.

We left Zalmoxis in the boot of the car, and went to see the tomb with its perfect blocks of dressed stone and the exquisite picture of the king on horseback that someone had painted in the third century BC. The guided tour lasted ten minutes, so short that it flattened the present moment to nothing, squashing it thinly between the future and the past so that it hardly existed. When we walked out of the tomb through its electronic sliding door, we were completely lost in time.

We drank another coffee in the exhibition space then threw away the plastic cup and stirrers and the ripped sugar packets.

'What about behind those display boards?' Claire said.

'They'll think it's rubbish.'

'Ssshhh she's looking.'

As another coach arrived, we drove out of the car park and followed the tourist trail past the ancient city of Helis, known to Greek scholars. This was supposed to be the place where the Getic king Dromichaetes dined with Lysimachos, heir to Alexander the Great, known around here as Alexander the Macedonian. We could have left the box there but it felt too dry and abandoned, even in the small temple by the gate where the archaeologists found the inscription to Phosphorus, the Greek god of cities. On the other side of the river the road rose up to a parking area where the oak trees shaded the tables and the bins overflowed with picnic rubbish. Here we were again at Demir Baba Tekke.

The trees along the path were tied with ribbons and scraps of cloth, even hats and baby clothes. All the way down the steps to the seven-sided mausoleum built for the Islamic mystic in Pythagorean geometry, on top of the

Thracian altar stones. The door of the old museum was so low that you had to bow to go inside. Pilgrims from all over the Balkans and Turkey had left ribbons on the grilled windows. Demir Baba was sacred to the Shia Muslims and to the thousands of Bulgarian Alevi who still lived in the villages around here. I wondered if Demir Baba himself knew anything about Zalmoxis from the classical sources that he must surely have read. Was that in fact the reason he had chosen this spot? The two sages were separated by 2000 years but they had a lot in common.

We drove round the back of the shrine where the lorries took away the bins full of coffee cups. Then we carried the box into the forest and left Zalmoxis at the bottom of the precinct wall. All over the stonework, there were fading inscriptions of symbols relating to the sun and the moon and the six pointed star of Solomon. Nobody can explain why there is such a crossover here between religions nor how the thread of folk sanctity has survived so long. One thing was clear. Unlike the national narrative which does little more than cement divisions between communities, the tomb of Demir Baba brings them all together, Christians, Muslims and even the agnostics.

For Zalmoxis, this place was far more suitable than our barn roof. The future was there, in the hopeful prayers of pilgrims. The past had a story too, it was alive. Even the present burst out occasionally when the families came to celebrate on *Gergiovden* according to the old calendar. Time was in balance and that was good for an immortal.

Was I ever going to find a future for myself? Smoking and drinking again in Troy's tiny house. At the end of that long winter it was still not clear but maybe the future was right there, in the episodes of Colombo on the screen of his laptop wired up to a home-made solar panel. Or Troy's rocket stove. If only we could see past all the ghosts.

I stumbled out a few hours later and shuffled down the hill wondering how the little god might be getting on in his box at the bottom of the Ottoman wall. I thought of the packet of Benson and Hedges, buried in that liminal spot on the other side of Europe, by the walled garden in Dalton and asked the air around me if there might still be a packet there, a time capsule, waiting like a hoard of Roman coins for the retrieval that never came.

18

Utopia

It was the first time I had seen any of them since winter.

'Now then everyone! Listen up! Here is somebody that will know what I'm talking about.' Walter said as I approached.

Sune and Troy were sitting around the outside table in the bar but nobody mentioned the wood. They all seemed to be getting on fine. The winter was like a forgotten dream. Walter thrust a full bottle of *Shumensko* at me,

'Chris, dear boy. Would you consider yourself to be a lotos eater?'

Roy lifted his head from the table, 'Fucksake. I still don't know what you're on about.'

'Calm down,' said Walter, 'Chris has been educated properly. In the English tradition. He is an archaeologist so will surely have read Homer. Chris, please enlighten us. With the notable exception of Hristo, thanks to his excellent state education, nobody here has any idea what I mean when I tell them they are all lotos eaters. Indolent, intoxicated and miles from home. The floor is yours, my man.'

There was a tinkle of lighters on bottle glass as a kind of drum roll so I stood up again.

'No idea,' I said and the table groaned as everyone clinked their bottles to mine and Walter slunk away defeated, leaving them free to talk about other matters.

Much later the same night, Walter caught up with me on the dark road home and we stood on the cooling tarmac and looked up at the stars.

'Are you pretending to be an ignoramus or does it come naturally?' he said. 'I thought you went to a good school?'

'I'm not sure it was a good school. Anyway, I never took any ancient Greek.'

'Eeee gods. Do me a favour. Go and do some reading. According to my understanding of Homer, we are all lotos eaters.'

'Because we got out of the rat race?'

'Just go and read some bloody books,' he said.

So, I did.

Homer's *Odyssey* is the epic story of Odysseus and his warriors, on their long voyage home after the Trojan War. In one of many adventures, they land on a strange island. When some of the men taste the fruit of the lotos tree they want nothing else but to stay where they are. Befuddled by the narcotic fruit, they lose the urge to return to Ithaca, until Odysseus forces them back onto the boat in chains. Homer's tale has endured and many writers have been inspired by the lotos eaters to create fables for their own times. Walter could see all of us reflected in there.

In 1935, Somerset Maugham published a short story called *The Lotus Eater*. An English banker Thomas Wilson leaves behind his comfortable suburban life and moves to the island of Capri so he can gaze all day at the gorgeous view which had so captivated him on holiday. He chooses idleness and beauty over salaried work and also vows to kill himself when the money runs out. Maugham was horrified by the idea of doing nothing for the sake of pleasure and he made sure that his protagonist died in madness and poverty. His story is a warning to anyone who dares to challenge the work ethic. Maugham saw the lotos eaters as a cautionary tale but most other authors have used it as a bohemian manifesto for individual freedom.

James Joyce, *Ulysses* is a mirror of *The Odyssey* and it's all about roots. Section five is called The Lotus Eaters too and in it, Bloom wanders the Dublin streets killing time before a funeral. Joyce conjures ideas of apathy, sleep and forgetfulness as well as the narcotic effects of Catholic ritual and the chemical compounds available in the chemist shops. Anything but work. Even though the book is all about Dublin, Joyce himself had left behind Ireland and was writing it as a cultural exile in Trieste and Zurich. The recycling of Homer's weird forgetful fruit has something to do with living away from home whether that home be Dublin, Ithaca or in my case, East Yorkshire.

Walter had no doubt read Joyce but there was another version that had probably influenced his thinking more, Alfred Lord Tennyson's long poem, *The Lotos Eaters*. In the poem, Tennyson gazes in awe at a foreign landscape where the red sun dips over outlandish nature and the trees are laden with mysterious fruit. With his back to Victorian England, he is reaching beyond the horizon for something exotic. In the original version, Homer briefly tempts us with the possibility of eternal apathy but then quickly snaps us back to duty and work. Tennyson is only interested in giving in to the bliss so, in his telling, the warriors do not go back to Ithaca at all. Instead, they remain on the island, forever doped up on some herbal strain of Xanax.

The lotos eaters story offers an alternative because it breaks those conceptions of time that we live by. In the UK, I had left behind a version of the future, embodied in a job for wages and career path but I was not sure with what I had replaced it. In the village, the dominant order of time was the endless cycles of seasons from winter to winter and from spring to spring but I had not signed up to that one either. I was living beside these calendars and chronologies, but stepping lightly over them to avoid their traps. It was no good trying to choose between the past, present and future because they all cease to exist as soon as you grab them. Even the present moment dissolves into a memory once you have put your attention on it. If the lotos eaters told me anything, it was that time means nothing at all. The lesson of that short clip from the mind of an ancient Greek story-teller and the truth in the numbing visions of those enlightened warriors was not to try and live in the present, but that time itself was essentially irrelevant. Being here in the village, with my office window facing the garden, watching the walnut tree change with the seasons, it feels like time does not affect us. Like Zalmoxis the cat, we are all immortal because it is only our bodies that will grow old and die.

But how did Walter translate all this to Bulgaria? The lotos eaters story is radically anti-provincial because it reveals another way of being. It puts before us, the idea of hedonism. We are free to do what we want. Life is short and should be sweet. I think Walter signed up to that. He wanted nothing more than to sail his yacht around the Aegean for the whole summer and in that sense, he was a lotos eater for the twenty first century. The rest of them had chosen to live here on a shoestring, drink cheap Bulgarian beer and forget all about going home so they were lotos eaters too.

Another anti-provincial influencer was the English poet, Robert Graves who moved to Deya in Mallorca in the mid 1920s and stayed there for the rest of his life writing books like *I Claudius* and *The White Goddess*. An idealist recovering from the existential shock of the First World War, he had moved away from England and made a place for himself in the sunshine. He remained there right up to his death in 1985, aged 90. Was he one as well?

Graves studied English literature and classics at Oxford and must have seen the Mediterranean sun, through Homer's eyes as well as through Tennyson's. For many English people, Greece and Spain were soaked in glamour. They held the possibility of permanent heavenly bliss, even apathy and intoxication if that is what you wanted. After the 1950s, these ancient stories inspired people to stay forever on their island, not as Maugham's character in degradation and loss but like Robert Graves in Deya, the Durrell family in Corfu or Leonard Cohen on the Greek island of Hydra, in freedom and peace and with abundance.

If I was a lotos eater, I had discovered the fruit as a teenager. It was on my doorstep. When I was 14, I found magic mushrooms in the field behind the church, so I made a pot of tea and sat down in the living room at Dalton to watch telly, with no idea what was about to happen. Mum came in with a basket of washing. She set up the ironing board behind me, as a feeling of pure delight spread up through unknown neural pathways to my head. Whenever I looked up, the light from the window fractured into tiny colourful cracks on the glass, like strands of rainbow tinted wire. I dragged my eyes away from the window. On the television was one of the grand train journeys of the world, The Devil's Nose in Ecuador and soon I had joined the rattling carriages winding through the Andes like a gigantic rollercoaster. I held on tightly to the chair in case I fell down the steep precipice into the gorge below. Mum's voice became like rushing water on the green mountain, or the whistling wind in the tops of the pines. I tried my best not to giggle but I could hardly contain the bubbling euphoria. From the very beginning, utopian feelings like these belonged to foreign places. They took me out of Dalton and beyond East Yorkshire to other worlds. Maybe that was when the journey began. I may have tasted the fruit but I had not yet found the island.

Years later, stumbling across a rave in a Welsh forest and being handed Ecstasy for the first time, I was doing it for real. Moving in the dark and the smoke, dancing inside a minute of techno as if it were the total sphere of the world and wanting to stay with that feeling forever, feet stamping on the ground and the stars above us. Some people I knew, one or two of my students even, dropped everything to stay with the travellers but I did not want to spend my days munching on pills and opium, so for me, once the eyes had opened, the radical notion was ditch the career path but choose to stay busy. Part of our motive for leaving the UK and going to Bulgaria was to free ourselves from paid work and to live by our own rules. Does that make us lotos eaters too?

I was drawn to the former eastern bloc because I believed, not in Lord Byron or Greek mythology, but in bands like the Fall and Joy Division. This was music that bounced off concrete walls and amplified the vitality of outsider spaces. I knew paradise was impossible but still I wanted to see Eastern Europe because it had been hidden from us for so long.

Bulgaria is no utopia but there are small luxuries here. We can leave the car unlocked on the streets of Sofia, walk for days in the hills between basic mountain lodges, ride on affordable grumbling trains, gaze at Byzantine frescoes and camp for free on deserted beaches. Like anarchists on the highway, we flash our lights to warn oncoming drivers to slow down because the police are waiting around the corner.

It's not what we imagined but there is a kind of solidarity and a long list of small freedoms. There are still things I miss from home like good butter and curry houses but mostly, I am happy to avoid Poppy Day, the royal family, endless announcements on expensive trains and the identical branded retail spaces in every single town: Greggs, Costa Coffee, Subway, Poundland and Currys.

I see the same people at Yanka's shop every morning and after ten years they shift up on the bench for me to sit down. In the centre, the men outside the Post Office look at me with faces that could be showing indifference. They shake their heads slightly, raising an eye lid but they don't say much. These men do not waste time with pleasantries but are always there if we need help to plough a garden or fix a car. The welcome we received from everyone is ongoing and genuine but I will always be a foreigner here. I have not become Bulgarian. I am still an Englishman abroad, whatever that means.

We came here on a radical mission but found ourselves doing the most traditional tasks in a thoroughly conservative village. Putting down roots in this rough-edged place was never easy but it was always fun. We made the guest house and I played in the band, we hosted workshops and organized holidays, we gave TV interviews and then later retreated into our own lives and the garden. In a sense we are still on the go, ready to leave again at the drop of a hat. By embracing our own scruffy utopia, we have become the ultimate lotos eaters, warmed by simple comforts and taking it easy whenever we can. Some days I worry about our precarious retirement but I am in no hurry to go back just yet.

From the garden we watch the seasons pass but we are not idle. The lotos fruit may have opened our hedonist eyes but there is always work to do, digging, planting, harvesting and that is what keeps us grounded. It is a paradise of our own design and in it, like Eden there are fruit trees. One of the oldest was an Apricot that Stoian Stoianov had planted just after the war. The 93-year-old diplomat had told us that himself. It was an old tree but we gave it a chance. I watched it over several years as it stopped producing fruit and finally decided to cut it down.

The job had three parts. Felling the tree, slicing through the trunk and branches to make logs and then trundling them all back to the shed. On the freshly cut trunk, the golden rings, uncountable, mapped year after year in the garden, 50, 60, 70 summers and winters. In every one, the tree had provided apricots for *rakia* and the tree rings showed it in their colours. Each ring had a different shade from pale single malt whiskey to barrel finished bourbon in dark hues of caramel and copper. I took a photo of the section to send to Stoianov in Greece hoping it would speak to him, like the end of a house or the end of a life. The kind of closure that might be peace-giving to an old man.

Like the tree rings, the garden was a calendar. Steady growth marked slow time in the spaces where we lived. The great walnut trees spread their leaves like lobes, branches, boughs, hovering over patches of grass. The shade growing all the time. Each year we made another compost heap, and the increasing row of mounds was like a landscape journal of the years. The garden's archaeology is still in motion and when you are part of it, the time passes slowly.

Eventually, Violeta died but it made no difference because every time I passed the place where she had always waited with her goats, she was still there. I saw her shuffling up the road with great dignity, her back bent forwards from the spine condition that had troubled her since childhood and which eventually killed her. I remembered the last time she was there, when her scarf was tied tightly against the wind. Petar was there too with a scythe in his hand but when he pushed it forwards at the long grass, the stalks just bent over and flattened down on the ground because the blade was so blunt.

'Petri, go back to bed. Light the *petchka* and lie down. Take a rest. Everything is too wet,' Violeta said.

He turned to me, '*Nyamam zhena nyamam pari* I have no woman, no money. No wife, no money,' and then he carried on up the street to the village centre wagging his finger at no one in particular as the dogs ran and barked behind him. That was the last time I saw her but Petar outlived them all.

I followed the herd to the bridge and then stopped beneath the poplars and watched the goats wander on towards the hill. The winter had bleached away the colours from the grass and the white fuzzy plum blossom looked like puffs of smoke scattered across the hillside. I could hear men's voices talking in staccato, half shouting. I scanned the hillside and hoped the great eye would stay closed this time. Maybe it was the Russian Cossacks walking on the battlefield or the partisans coming down from the forests? Thank God for that. It was only the tractor driver on a call, his voice carrying across the vast acres of silence to bounce off the hill, half a kilometre from his machine. So, I turned back to the village and the sweet quick smell of Spring. A stork was poking the ground with its beak looking for worms in the soil and when I stopped to watch the elegance of its long legs, a golden oriole busted out its warbling song like a crazy flute. From the hedgerow, Belcho gave a couple of barks. Had he found Wally's last place or was he just scouting for his own?

The frost had exposed the limestone blocks stacked like loaves of bread below the road. Every time there was heavy rain the mud washed down over them and in winter the frost broke open the thin tarmac crust above. The surface was fractured but nothing was going to break the chunks of limestone at the base. I turned away from the stratigraphy and the stork and stepped on back to the village to see finally, what was left of the future and the journey to somewhere else.

A Final Word
Breakfast on 7 January 2023

A year later, I am in the west. A seasonal worker in the French Alps, making breakfast every day for the ski groups. Through the chalet window, I watch the sun come up over Mont Blanc and I know that my old friend Dimo is starting his day with a *rakia* because, in Bulgaria, it is *Ivanovden* and that was his father's name day. Laying out the bowls and jars for the tourists takes me back there. In France the breakfast ingredients come from the supermarket but in Podgoritsa, the honey, the walnuts and yoghurt were part of the place. My old Bulgarian village was nothing without them. The raw milk came from Bogdan and Fatme's cows and I always had to wait on the bench outside the milking shed, sitting there sometimes for a whole hour. These two may have been farmers but they were not early risers. Bogdan's mum would walk past and shrug, tapping the watch on her wrist. Other men came up with plastic bottles for filling and all of them, Pesho,

Gosho, and Dimo himself said it was good milk *hubavo mlyako*. They knew each of the cows by name. Back home, with the warm milk, I would make yoghurt, enough for three days.

The honey came from Stefan bees. *Pchelnik*. A bee man. One of several back then, but these days who knows how many there are left? The taste of his honey altered throughout the year. Stefan always said that springtime Acacia was the best but everyone had their favourite. Just like the tree rings, each type was a different shade of copper.

In early Autumn, the walnuts dropped from six huge trees that surrounded the garden. Enormous, they towered over the puny apples. Those walnut trees were at least 100 years old, a good age for this place of ruins and in better shape than most of the houses. The canopies were home to golden orioles and woodpeckers, red squirrels and scampering *belki*. In September we gathered the nuts and stored them in big sealed containers for the year then saved the cappuccino-coloured shells for the fire. That was the nature of breakfast in my former home. A world away from this high-end ski resort. I wonder if the men are all still going to the farm, sitting quietly by the gate, Bogdan and Fatme snoring until 9 am. The last time I was there, I scanned the houses facing me, all along the meadow and tried to commit the whole scene to memory. All I can see now are the black ribbons gathered up on the doors like curious bows on gothic gifts, pinned to the painted wood by sons and daughters to mark the death of each final resident, to close up the houses in this resilient village. Like no other place I have ever seen. Even for me, an archaeologist and folk horror fan, the overwhelming weight of the past and the un-attended litter of ruins was, after 15 years, just too much.

The German family are getting ready to go skiing and as I wash up the breakfast things, I want to go back to Bulgaria and see for myself, but all I can do is find five minutes to call Dimo.

'Happy name day for your dad,' I say,

'*Kude si?*' Where are you?' he replies,

'In the French Alps. Skiing. Living the dream.'

'*Bravo momche,*'

'*Ciao* Dimo, see you soon.'

I gaze out of the window at the distant peaks like toblerone wedges, shimmering in the bright morning sun and then go back to work, coating the beef in flour and browning the chunks of meat for the *Bourgignon*.

Acknowledgements

My biggest thank you is to Claire who has shared the journey. Without her, none of it would ever have happened. She has always been there for me with love, strength, good vibes and wise counsel. Thank you, petal!

The following people have been friends and helpers along the way. Thanks to all of them (in no particular order): Mitko, Diana, Stela, Yuliana, Milcho, Plamen, Rumi, Kathy, Elly, Dancho, Andrew G and Ady, Paul and Emma, Mel and Paul, Iva, Paul (gasifier), Ray, Naiden, Ivanichka, Ivo (Dkstrkt), Nadia V, Ivo (Gips), Raul, Steve and Sharon, Lisa and Ewen, Gosho and Annie, Sonny and Charlotte, Tui, Mark and Cara, Viv and Steve, Bogomil and Natalya, Boggie, Petar, Collio, Albena, Safi, Mersin, Yilko, Yomer, Mustafa and Remsie, Aziz, Krasen, Jordy and Jenny, Chris and Norman, Yvonne and Martin, Julie S, Stela S, Trudie, Nkiru, Maya, Erin, Andrew for the Man Days, Tracy, Ian, Dale and Stephen, Margaret, Rod and Anne, Stuart and Helen, Maria, Petar and Lubo (PC Health), Jason, Daniela, Roger, Tony and Carol, Joe and Julie, June and George, Dr Neli and all our house sitters, guests and volunteers especially James W, Tracy, Guillaume and Natacha, Moon and James M.

Nazdrave to the ones who are no longer with us: Hristana, Ivanka, Netzer, Stoian, Nedyalka, Rumi, Justine, Pesho (maistor), Pesho (gadulka), Gary, Jock, Keith, Davey, Dobri, David, Patsy, Olivia, Peter (Posabina), Uche.

I want to thank the Elizabeth Kostova Foundation for giving me a chance in 2017 as a Fellow at the Sozopol Seminar for Creative Non-Fiction, namely Elizabeth Kostova, Milena Deleva, Philip Graham, Simona Ilieva and Violeta Radkova and for all kinds of wonderful support since then. I am also grateful to Dimana Trankova and Anthony Georgieff of Vagabond Media for publishing my stories and to Nowhere Magazine for printing 'Stoian' and awarding it the prize which gave me so much hope. I am grateful to Diana Ivanova and Eireene Nealand for timely advice and for introducing me to the Goat Milk festival. Thanks also to Maya, Ewen and the gang at *Yovchevata Kushta*, Elena for space in which I could write. Thanks also to all the English Boarding School Survivors who have opened up in public and in the media. Hearing other people's experiences has helped to validate and acknowledge my own.

All kinds of people have taken time to read different versions of the text and given support and feedback. This has helped so much in getting the text in shape. Thanks to Lesley Bryce, Alba Z B, Peter Swainson, Tom Phillips, Dina Iordanova, Nadezhda Vassileva, Susan Curtis of Istros Books, Peter Fenton, Lisa O'Brien, Andrew Robinson, Helen Conway, Kapka Kassabova and Claire Coulter. The cover design was done by geneva_art and the Fimber Press logo was by Pinar Yildiz.

Special thanks to Kapka Kassabova whose encouraging words set me on this track in the first place. Her fantastic books, unfailing generosity, support and encouragement over the last ten years has kept me working.

A final word of thanks to the two women who inspired this writing. Ana, our neighbour of fifteen years who still looks, not a day over 35 and to the memory of Nedyalka, a truly independent spirit. The three of us used to wait for the goats together every day. They did the talking, I did the listening. The two women in the book, Violeta and Simona are based on these two but some of the stories in these pages are from other people entirely.

Big up the grandkids, Lily, Zeffi, Rudy, Sunniva and Koa, les Poeufs (Alex, Josh, Max, Sophie, Hannah, Marley), the brothers gonna walk it out (Kim, Jaq, Peter, Lisa, Nick and Winnie) and the ones we all miss: gran, mum, dad, Carol and Charles. My family have always been great travellers so thanks also to John, Julie and Sallie for the continuing inspiration.

The text is a story based on real events and lived experience but the writing reflects my own personal perspective, imagination and memory. The characters are created from real people but I have changed their names and I have also changed the name of the village.

Selected Sources

John Bell, *Peasants in Power: Alexander Stamboliiski and the Bulgarian Agrarian National Union, 1899-1923.* Princeton University Press

Peter J Conradi, *A Very English Hero: The Making of Frank Thompson.* Bloomsbury

Richard Crampton, *A Concise History of Bulgaria.* Cambridge University Press

Richard Crampton, *Aleksandur Stamboliiski.* Haus Publishing

Gerald Creed, *Domesticating Revolution: From Socialist Reform to Ambivalent Transition in a Bulgarian Village.* Penn State University Press

Raymond Detrez, *Historical Dictionary of Bulgaria.* Rowman and Littlefield

Minoo Dinshaw, *Outlandish Knight: The Byzantine Life of Steven Runciman.* Allen Lane

Anthony Georgieff, Dimana Trankova and Bozhidar Aleksiev, *The Turks of Bulgaria: History, Traditions, Culture.* Vagabond Media

Anthony Georgieff and Dimana Trankova, *A Guide to Communist Bulgaria Vols 1-3.* Free Speech International

Anthony Georgieff and Dimana Trankova, *Vagabond Magazine*, to 2024

Diana Georgieva, *The Archaeological Reserve at Sboryanovo.*

Misha Glenny, *The Balkans 1804-1999: Nationalism, War and the Great Powers.* Granta Books

Peter Heather and John Matthews, *The Goths in the Fourth Century.* Liverpool University Press

Herodotus, *The Histories.* Penguin Classics

RF Hoddinott, *The Thracians.* Thames and Hudson

Homer, *The Odyssey.* Penguin Classics

Rumen Ivanov, *Roman Cities in Bulgaria vol 1.* Prof Marin Drinov Academic Publishing House

James Joyce, *Ulysses.* Wordsworth

Hristo Karastoyanov, *The Same Night Awaits Us All.* Open Letter

Kapka Kassabova, *Border: A Journey to the Edge of Europe.* Granta Books

Kapka Kassabova, *Street Without a Name: Childhood and Other Misadventures in Bulgaria.* Granta Books

Patrick Leigh Fermor, *The Broken Road. From the Iron Gates to Mount Athos.* John Murray Press

Mercia MacDermot, *Once Upon a time in Bulgaria.* Manifesto Press Cooperative

Mercia MacDermot, *The Apostle of Freedom: a portrait of Vasil Levsky against a background of nineteenth century Bulgaria.* Allen and Unwin

Somerset Maugham, *Collected Short Stories vol 4.* Vintage

Geo Milev, *Once There Was Spring: Poems and Prose-Poems.* trans. Tom Phillips. Worple Press

Alfred Lord Tennyson, *An Outstanding Collection of his best loved Poems.* Weidenfeld and Nicholson

Ivaylo Znepolski, Mihail Gruev, Momchil Metodiev, Martin Ivanov, Daniel Vatchkov, Ivan Elenkov, Plamen Doynov, *Bulgaria under Communism.* Routledge

Пламен Събев (Plamen Sabev), *Паламарца: едно капанско село. (Palamartsa: A Kapantsi village).* Зограф (Zograf)

Пламен Събев (Plamen Sabev), *Големите военни маневри край попово (Military Manouevres at Popovo),* Исторически музей попово

Author photo by Kim Fenton

Christopher Fenton worked as an archaeologist for twenty years in UK before heading out to Bulgaria with his wife Claire in 2010. As a writer in the academic field (Chris Fenton-Thomas), he published books and articles on landscape archaeology. In Bulgaria he began to study creative writing especially poetry and non-fiction and has published a number of short pieces with Vagabond Magazine (Sofia) and Nowhere Magazine (New York). In 2017 he was a Fellow at the Sozopol Seminar for Creative Non-Fiction run by the Elizabeth Kostova Foundation. For ten years he ran a guest house and smallholding in Bulgaria but since the Covid 19 pandemic, has worked in various jobs including online English teacher, chalet host in the French Alps and personal support worker in social care in Essex. Chris has three sons and five grandchildren. He is currently working on writing projects about the east coast of England including family heritage and maritime history around the port of Hull. His home is in Bulgaria.

www.christopherfentonwritings.com

instagram name: christopherfentonwritings

Printed in Dunstable, United Kingdom